HOW DID JESUS WANT THE EUCHARIST?

HOW DID JESUS WANT THE EUCHARIST?

Looking Back to Find a Way Forward

ANSGAR WUCHERPFENNIG, SJ

Translated by Patrick Conlin

Paulist Press
New York / Mahwah, NJ

Cover image by Adam Ján Figel' / Alamy.com
Cover design by Joe Gallagher
Book design by Lynn Else

Library of Congress Cataloging-in-Publication Data
Names: Wucherpfennig, Ansgar, 1965– author.
Title: How did Jesus want the Eucharist?: looking back to find a way forward / Ansgar Wucherpfennig ; translated by Patrick Conlin.
Other titles: Wie hat Jesus Eucharistie gewollt? English
Description: New York; Mahwah, NJ: Paulist Press, [2024] | Includes bibliographical references. | Summary: "This book investigates scripture and history to show that the role of women, ministry, and ecumenism in the Eucharist must be rethought"—Provided by publisher.
Identifiers: LCCN 2023057117 (print) | LCCN 2023057118 (ebook) | ISBN 9780809156825 (paperback) | ISBN 9780809188468 (ebook)
Subjects: LCSH: Lord's Supper. | Lord's Supper—Biblical teaching.
Classification: LCC BV825.3 .W8313 2024 (print) | LCC BV825.3 (ebook) | DDC 234/.163—dc23/eng/20240412
LC record available at https://lccn.loc.gov/2023057117
LC ebook record available at https://lccn.loc.gov/2023057118

ISBN 978-0-8091-5682-5 (paperback)
ISBN 978-0-8091-8846-8 (ebook)

Published by Paulist Press
997 Macarthur Boulevard
Mahwah, New Jersey 07430
www.paulistpress.com

Printed and bound in the
United States of America

CONTENTS

FOREWORD

THE CELEBRATION OF the Eucharist, especially the Sunday celebration, is often described in summary as the "source and summit" of our faith. Drawing on the theology presented in the Second Vatican Council's Constitution on the Sacred Liturgy, *Sacrosanctum Concilium*, these three words—"source and summit"—bear considerable meaning and convey the profundity with which Christians approach the celebration of the Lord's Supper. In an age when mass-produced wheat wafers are the norm for "bread" and communion under both kinds is an increasing rarity in many parishes, particularly after the COVID-19 pandemic, any resemblance between an authentic "supper" composed of recognizable food and drink and the modern celebration of the Eucharist can be challenging to find. This is not a new phenomenon. If one reflects on the post-Tridentine, preconciliar celebration of the Eucharist, which was prayed in a dead language with the presider's back to a largely passive congregation that would later receive communion without ever touching it and while kneeling, there is an even starker disconnect between the paschal meal inaugurated by Jesus of Nazareth on the night before he died and what Christians have been doing in memory of him.

In addition to the experiential incongruence between the Lord's Supper and the modern celebration of the Eucharist, there is also the widespread lack of historical and theological knowledge about the origins, history, and meaning of this sacred celebration. Over my years of teaching theology and exercising pastoral ministry, I have encountered not a few Christians who think that what Jesus and his closest followers did in the upper room on Holy Thursday was an exact play-for-play reflection of what they do each Sunday. Jesus put on vestments like their local pastor, spoke prayers in the same way as their modern presider, and had eucharistic elements and sacred vessels that looked like what they see in the sanctuary today. On the one hand, such an anachronistic imagination is absurd. And yet, on the other hand, our catechesis, religious education, and practices of ongoing mystagogy are often so insufficient that parishioners are largely left to their own devices to conjure up what it must have been like, insofar as they even think about the origins of the Eucharist.

For this reason, this book by Ansgar Wucherpfennig is a welcome and refreshing resource for anybody interested in learning more about not only the origins of the Eucharist but also what early Christian communities witnessed to in their own reception and practice of the Lord's Supper. Biblical scholars and historical theologians alike have long noted that meals are a central and important part of Jesus's earthly ministry. Sharing a meal presumes some level of intimacy and vulnerability. One must put down their guard, expose their finitude and dependence on others for sustenance and survival. It is for this reason that so many deep conversations take place over shared meals, and why meals are often central in the key moments of human life: births, deaths, weddings, birthdays, and so on. God incarnate, Jesus of Nazareth, ministers to friends and strangers alike over shared meals and invites his followers to continue that practice. It is also within that context of the eucharistic meal that Christ promises to remain present to the Church.

What we see from the outset in Wucherpfennig's historical survey of the early Church and its celebration of the Lord's Supper in various geographic locations and among a range of early Christian communities, is the diversity of its content and style. One of the interesting details about the early Christian practice of the Lord's Supper is the range of elements that were involved in the eucharistic meal. For example, the testimony of the third-century text called the *Apostolic Tradition* explains that, in addition to bread and wine, cheese and olives were offered as part of the Eucharist at an episcopal ordination. To some modern readers this might seem strange, or even "sacrilegious," but one thing it absolutely does is convey the reality of a meal. We know that the original Lord's Supper, which is recounted as a Passover feast, certainly had more elements than merely bread and wine. While nobody is advocating for a change in today's eucharistic elements, the history of the celebration's development does encourage us to remember Jesus's earthly meal ministry and to recall that what we do in liturgy has its origins in that very practical and earthly outreach.

At the end of this study, Wucherpfennig notes that the "variability and variety of the sacred meal in the first Christian congregations does not reveal any final and complete form of the celebration of the Eucharist." Rather than see this as a sign for despair or frustration, he argues that there are ecumenical implications to be found here. The range of traditions for celebrating the Lord's Supper, dating back to that first Holy Thursday meal, invites us to expand our contemporary horizons to recognize the ways one may continue to find a sense of unity amid such diversity. There are many implications that arise from a reading of the early history of the Eucharist. For example, what is essential and what is extraneous? What is the range of diverse and regionally or culturally specific adaptations that can be included or modified? Who ought to preside at the eucharistic meal and what are the ministerial and liturgical roles to be included in such a celebration? What is the function of the homily in expressing the prophetic call that Christians receive at baptism? And who may be permitted to preach and why?

This small book does not provide answers to all these questions, but it does give readers much food for thought. It will be challenging for some, affirming for others, yet enlightening for all. And the questions and topics it inspires for discussion will surely deepen every reader's appreciation for the history and lived practice of the Eucharist.

Daniel P. Horan, OFM

INTRODUCTION

THE GOSPELS ARE written from the experience of the risen Jesus. They remember Jesus not as a dead man from the past, but as one presently living, including in the Eucharist. *The Church celebrates the Eucharist because in it, the Risen One reminds the Church that he is alive.* "How did the risen Jesus want the Eucharist?" is the better question. A purely historical inquiry will only produce modest results. The theological task is to understand the exciting unity in the early Christian testimonies. The diversity of their views and representations is not an obstacle, but rather is a richness that can both be useful and bring great joy. This is true not only for the Gospels, but for other early Christian writings as well. They, too, bear witness to Jesus, the risen and living Messiah, and the continuation of his earthly ministry. Therefore, in my search for an answer to the question of how the Risen One wanted the Eucharist, I did not want to start with the pre-resurrection Jesus of around the year 30. Instead, I slowly work backward from the many early Christian testimonies about the Eucharist in the second and third centuries to the pre-Easter origins of the Eucharist. In this way, it will become clear that Christians were guided by the inspiration of the risen Christ, both in the celebration of the Eucharist and the search for its form.

By "Eucharist," I am referring to the Christian sacrament of the Lord's Supper. The word *eucharist* does not yet occur with Jesus himself, so the question of how he wanted the Eucharist is admittedly anachronistic. Johannes zu Eltz, the dean of Frankfurt, first asked me this question, looking for a statement to give to a meeting of the Frankfurt synodal council in preparation for Ökumenischer Kirchentag 2021.[1] Although I am writing this book as a Catholic and limiting myself to the "Eucharist," this is not in opposition to the "Lord's Table" in Lutheran (Protestant) churches. Rather, I have not given up waiting and hoping that Protestant and Catholic Christians can celebrate "together at the Lord's table."[2] The first reflections for this book arose in a "Frankfurt Ecumenical Circle" of practical and systematic theologians, in which we ascertained what the Lord's Supper and the Eucharist means to us in terms of a common celebration. A communion at the table of the Lord that unites churches could give Christians the strength to face the increasingly urgent social, political, economic, and ecological questions of today together. This is the goal with which I approached the question of how Jesus intended the Eucharist, and I am happy if my reflections can contribute to its implementation.

Despite some misgivings, I find the question "How did Jesus want the Eucharist?" satisfactory in its conciseness. The very question assumes that the later celebration of the Eucharist developed from a foundational idea in the life of Jesus. Churches across denominational lines hold fast to the confessional belief that Jesus celebrated the Lord's Supper, or the Eucharist, as a sacrament. This foundational idea for the Eucharist would not have been possible without the earlier, historical meal of Jesus. The Eucharist came into being after Easter; its theological meaning, though, belongs to the middle of Jesus's life, not its end. Based on this insight, John the Evangelist placed his eucharistic tradition in the middle of Jesus's life. In the Capernaum synagogue, John has Jesus speak some of the most offensive words of his life, "For my flesh is true food and my blood is true drink. Those who eat my flesh and drink my blood abide in me, and I in them" (John 6:55–56).[3]

EVERY COOKING POT IS SACRED...

In terms of religious history, Jesus and the "kingdom of God" movement, which came to be synonymous with his name, stand in the tradition of sacred meals—holy mealtimes.[4] The Eucharist is fundamentally about eating and drinking. Gottfried Bachl writes in his book on the Eucharist, "The Godhead gives itself, its Word and Being, in such a way that, the particular human condition in every aspect becomes salutary and comprehensible, even our need to eat and drink."[5] Bachl explains how Jesus understood eating and drinking as his mission and defended himself against the slander that he was a friend of the wrong people, "a glutton and a drunkard."[6] In both regular meals and in the holy meal, Jesus "is not concerned with any grace except that which comes through the concrete codes of nourishing and consuming."[7]

Jesus's understanding of the holiness of a meal is both extensive and intensive. Extensive, because Jesus includes diverse forms of eating, drinking, and the ordinariness associated with them in his proclamation of the kingdom of God. The end of the Book of Zechariah says, "And every cooking pot in Jerusalem and Judah shall be sacred to the LORD of hosts, so that all who sacrifice may come and use them to boil the flesh of the sacrifice. And there shall no longer be traders in the house of the LORD of hosts on that day" (Zech 14:21). Jesus knew the end of Zechariah. The last sentence of the book was the impulse for him to expel the merchants from the temple. In the prophetic vision, the holiness of the sacrificial meals spreads from the temple to every pot and bowl in the whole country; a holy meal is cooking on every hearth. Jesus was similar to these Jewish movements that did not limit human holiness to the temple district but extended it to the country and the people.

At the same time, Jesus's understanding of sacred meals is *intensive*. He could see signs of God's nearness even in mundane aspects of the meal. In the activity of a woman baking bread and in the miracle of dough rising, the kingdom of God becomes tangible (cf. Matt 13:33). Four of his parables in Matthew 13:1–35 are about fruits of the earth: two about grain, one about the mustard seed, and one about leaven. They all cause one to marvel at the wonders of the earth, which, despite every obstacle, produces fruits to feed people and plants that, as in the parable of the mustard seed, even give dwelling to the birds of the sky. Even the grain of wheat, from which the flour for the bread on the tables is ground, becomes a prophetic image for Jesus's own death: "Unless a grain of wheat falls into the earth and dies, it remains just a single grain; but if it dies, it bears much fruit" (John 12:24). Death is not annihilation. This grain of wheat from heaven does not die in order to perish, but rather for the sake of a new, relational life.

The Gospels set these words of Jesus in new contexts. It is quite possible that he originally said them during a meal. As the people saw and tasted the goodness of the LORD (Ps 34:8), Jesus proclaimed God's nearness to them. In the early Christian gatherings, prophets would share a word at the holy meal. They shared their insights during the meal and gave the meal theological interpretations with their images and admonitions. This is also true of Jesus; *Jesus saw himself as a prophet (Mark 6:4). He sanctified communal eating and drinking as the place of his proclamation.*

MORE THAN IN THE UPPER ROOM

The Christian celebration of the Eucharist developed from Jewish and Hellenistic traditions that predate Christianity. In thinking about Jesus and the Eucharist, theology often limits its view to the events in the Upper Room. In doing so, the range that the celebration had in its beginnings is lost. This range cannot have come from the Upper Room alone. Certainly, the great liturgies—not only the Lutheran and Catholic celebrations of the Last Supper, but also the Divine Liturgy of John Chrysostom in the Eastern churches—commemorate the Last Supper of Jesus with his disciples. But in none of these traditions is the liturgy merely an imitation of what Jesus did with his disciples.

For the Lutheran liturgy of the Lord's Supper, the words of institution are "konstitutive" (constitutive)[8] components of every eucharistic celebration, together with the Lord's Prayer, the distribution of the elements, and the thanksgiving prayer. According to the Augsburg Confession, the Lord's Supper is to be administered as a sacrament "according to the Gospel."[9] The traditional preface prayer of the Lutheran liturgy expands the horizon of the events of the Last Supper. In the preface, the congregation joins in the praise of all creation with the Trisagion, the Thrice Holy. All rulers, authorities, powers, and forces that still now oppress the community, will also fall in the eschatological Trisagion. Thus, the preface in the liturgical guide of the Evangelical Lutheran Church in Hesse and Nassau (EKHN) reads,

"Therefore the angels praise your glory, the powers worship you, and all the authorities fear you. The powers of heaven praise you with unanimous exultation and confess without end, 'Holy, holy, holy....'"[10]

In the Catholic Liturgy of the Eucharist, the commemoration of Jesus's Last Supper is underscored by the gestures of the priest-celebrant. After the words "This is my body," he lifts up the bread and shows it to the congregation and after the words "This is the chalice of the blood of the new and eternal covenant," he raises the chalice as well. He venerates both with a bow or genuflection. But the words that recall the meal of Jesus are not a reenactment. They are embedded in a prayer of utmost theological significance addressed to God. This prayer asks for God's Spirit, who is the actual active person in the liturgical event. God acts in the Eucharist through his Spirit, or better, through the power of the Holy Spirit that transforms our reality—to use more biblical language. For the Bible does not conceive of the Holy Spirit as a ghostly apparition or a specter, but as a force or power that people feel and that unites them to God.

In the part of the Eucharistic Prayer liturgically and theologically known as the epiclesis ("calling down"), the priest says, "Make holy, therefore, these gifts, we pray, by sending down your Spirit upon them like the dewfall, so that they may become for us the Body and Blood of our Lord Jesus Christ."[11] With the power of his Spirit, God extends the table of his Son to such an extent that there are innumerably more people at it than there were who gathered around him at the Last Supper. They gather with the whole of creation in a common sacrifice of praise for God. Thus, the third Eucharistic Prayer says, "You are indeed holy, O Lord, and all you have created rightly gives you praise, for through your Son our Lord Jesus Christ, by the power and working of the Holy Spirit, you give life to all things and make them holy, and you never cease to gather a people to yourself, so that from the rising of the sun to its setting a pure sacrifice may be offered to your name."

Therefore, I do not begin my following exegetical reflections on the beginnings of the Eucharist with the Upper Room but move backward from the second and third centuries to its origins with Jesus. Our journey begins in the first chapter with a *tour d'horizon* along the broad panorama of its early Christian forms in post-New Testament times. Then, in the second chapter, I will examine a relatively late New Testament writing, the Revelation to John, for its eucharistic testimony. It may seem that I give disproportionate space to it here; nevertheless, it deserves greater attention in the broader discussion of the Eucharist. For a Christian in the current global situation, this text is particularly meaningful with its visions of worldwide catastrophes and diseases. The following third chapter deals with the *Didache*, the "Teaching of the Twelve Apostles." Although this early church order did not find its way into the New Testament, it was written at about the same time as the later New Testament texts and is an important witness to the development of the Eucharist in New Testament times. In the last two chapters, I come to the tradition of the Last Supper and the post-Easter development of the celebration of the Eucharist, so as to finally scrutinize today's eucharistic practice based on the exegetical evidence.

ACKNOWLEDGMENTS

I WOULD LIKE to say a heartfelt εὐχαριστῶ (thank you) to those with whom I have experienced important moments of fellowship around the Lord's table in recent years: the university community and the Jesuits of Sankt Georgen, the Frankfurt Lutheran Congregation of the Redeemer, and the religious orders of the Little Sisters of Jesus and the Benedictine Sisters in Eibingen.

I would like to thank Anne-Katrin Helms, Johannes zu Eltz, and Klaus Vechtel. They proofread the manuscript in different phases and helped me with their comments and questions. Burkhard Menke accompanied the creation of the manuscript for the Patmos publishing house with gentle perseverance.

I owe it to the exchange in the extended Frankfurt ecumenical circle that I was able to think about and discuss many things in this book: Anne-Katrin Helms, Achim Knecht, Andrea Kortus, Gabriele and Peter Scherle, Martin Vorländer, Klaus Vechtel, and Johannes zu Eltz.

1

BREAD, WINE, OLIVES, AND MUCH MORE

GOTTFRIED BACHL NOTES that "Jesus uses the elements of nature to demonstrate the presence of the Kingdom of God. The Passover lamb that he ate every year, the food at banquets and wedding feasts, fish and honey, bread and wine at the Lord's Supper, all represent the created world which sustains human life."[1] Fish, honey, bread, and wine all became for Jesus and nascent Christianity the sign of new life from God through a meal. Strikingly, however, the Gospels never mention Jesus eating the Passover lamb. Only once in the Gospels does Jesus celebrate the Passover meal and they do not speak of the Passover lamb. In general, meat is absent from the *cuisine de sacrifice*[2] at the eucharistic meal of the first centuries. From its beginnings, the Eucharist is a feast that frees people from the compulsion to "eat each other in social situations."[3] In the Eucharist, the vicious circle is broken by eating and drinking, from which "life itself... [comes] from life that has been killed and slaughtered."[4]

THE EUCHARIST REDUCED TO GLUTTONY

In time, as the Eucharist was established as a distinct sacrament, it was celebrated as ritualized eating and drinking of dry bread and wine, as Jesus is reported to have done at the Last Supper.[5] More nourishing, full meals were also held in relation to this. This development, however, only emerges in the third century. In the beginning, bread and wine were usually the essential foods at the Eucharist, but not everywhere. In the early days, bread and wine were not taken as symbolic food in a ritualized meal, but as a main meal that would satisfy one's hunger. A special bread and a special chalice were emphasized by the prayer, but there were other breads and chalices that were distributed at the meal.

However, bread and wine were often accompanied by other side dishes. In Greek, *opson* or *optos* (literally "roasted" or "cooked") referred to anything that was eaten with the bread—most simply salt but also other dishes that were eaten alongside the main staple, for example, fried fish. According to Luke, the disciples gave such a side dish of fish to the risen Jesus when he appeared to them in Jerusalem and asked for something to eat. Bread, side dishes (*opson*), and wine—these were the three common parts of a meal in the early Christian environment. Some manuscripts also mention a honeycomb as part of the meal with the fish (see Luke 24:42–43 KJV).

At the baptismal Eucharist, in addition to bread and wine, milk and honey might also be enjoyed as a reminder of the biblical promise to Israel to have a land flowing with milk and honey. According to the early third-century church order known as the *Apostolic Tradition*, during an episcopal ordination, cheese and olives are offered along with bread and wine. A prayer here asks for nonmaterial gifts from God with these two gifts of nature, "Sanctify this milk that has been united into one mass and unites us to thy love. Let thy loving kindness ever rest upon this fruit of the olive, which is a type of thy bounty, which thou didst cause to flow from the tree unto life for them who hope on thee."[6]

However, there is also a conspicuous blank space in the variety of eucharistic foods that have been handed down: *meat is not documented in the surviving early Christian testimonies of the eucharistic meal.* This might recall the first commandment about food in the Bible which prescribes a vegetarian diet. The end of the first account of creation says, "See, I have given you every plant yielding seed that is upon the face of all the earth, and every tree with seed in its fruit; you shall have them for food" (Gen 1:29). Humans, animals of the earth, and birds of the sky all receive the same meatless nourishment from God.

The Pythagoreans already established philosophical reasons for abstaining from meat in pre-Christian times. However, this can also be found in the Jewish environment of nascent Christianity. The Jewish philosopher Philo of Alexandria wrote about a group called the "Therapeutae." This was a Jewish movement that had withdrawn from urban civilization. Female Therapeutae are specifically named, since both women and men belonged to this movement of urban withdrawal. Philo explains that their name carries the double meaning of *therapeuein.* It means both healing *and* service before God. The word is also frequently used to describe Jesus treating and healing diseases. Female and male Therapeutae retreated from large cities because they rejected the elaborate banquets that occurred there, and the luxury associated with the cities in general. They lived in austere homes in the healthy, fresh air by a lake near

Alexandria. They did not allow slaves to serve them their meals. They rejected slavery as unnatural because all human beings are born free by nature. Injustice and greed have tempted people to oppress their own kind as slaves. According to their ideals of a natural, healthy life, they renounced all meat at meals. They ate their bread with salt and hyssop sauce. In addition, they only drank the "clearest water," usually cold, with warm water reserved only for older men who were previously used to more luxurious lives.[7]

The Jewish-Christian historian Hegesippus also reported that renunciation of meat was part of the way of life for James, the "brother of the Lord." He was stoned to death in Jerusalem around AD 63 and the New Testament preserves a letter bearing his name. According to Hegesippus, James did not eat meat and subjected himself to strict asceticism. He drank no wine, he let no razor touch his head, he did not anoint himself with oil, and he did not bathe. His way of life must have been exemplary for a large group of Christians, because the First Letter to Timothy shows a debate against similar ideas. Timothy is advised to drink not only water but also some wine "for the sake of your stomach and your frequent ailments" (1 Tim 5:23). This admonition is probably not only for Timothy, but for a Christian movement that rejected wine as a sign of excessive luxury.

It is not clear whether James, despite his abstinence, drank wine at the eucharistic meal at least. However, the use of a chalice of water instead of wine at the Eucharist in early Christianity is evident in an ascetic movement attested to in various places. Early Christians knew them as "Encratites," from the Greek word for "self-control" or "abstinence" (*enkrateia*). According to the sources, many women were Encratites in addition to men. In many cases, Encratites not only abstained from alcohol, but also from meat. They represented, therefore, a progression from the previously mentioned Jewish and Greek philosophical movements.

The words of Jesus to the Samaritan woman at Jacob's well were not interpreted in Encratite circles as referring to baptism but to the Eucharist, "but those who drink of the water that I will give them will never be thirsty. The water that I will give will become in them a spring of water gushing up to eternal life" (John 4:14). Since Jesus spoke of drinking water, they understood Jesus to mean that he had a chalice of water at the Eucharist.

Encratites, like the Jewish Therapeutae, combined critical views of society with their asceticism. They refused to accept the mechanisms of the ancient economy and entertainment that destroyed human life. With their austere way of life, they protested against the disturbing experiences of violence in everyday life, from the enslavement of men and women to public spectacles. Tatian, a Syrian Christian, for example, formulated his criticism of the "bread and circus" politics of Rome in the middle of the second century, "You slaughter animals to eat their flesh and you buy men for the soul's cannibalistic feast, to feed them the most impious bloodshed. The robber murders in order to plunder, but the rich buy gladiators just to be killed."[8]

With the dramatic image of "the soul's cannibalistic feast," Tatian condemns the public spectacle of the Roman games, which by the imperial period had become a bloody and bestial spectacle. But he also exposes a meal culture that all too often costs sacrifices that remain hidden from the diners, and not only in antiquity. Eating and drinking has always involved cycles of violence. To "demolish" something is a vulgar way to express that one has eaten it. According to the Bible, in Paradise, no living beings were to be demolished or destroyed for food, implying a vegetarian diet. The Eucharist preserved this Edenic food culture. The history of human eating and drinking is accompanied by the constant threat of cultural loss. On the one hand, the ascetic way of life of the Encratite movement opposed the widespread exploitation of humans and nature. On the other hand, it emphasized the creaturely bond between humans and animals.

THE EUCHARIST IN THE *ACTS OF PHILIP*

The relationship between humans and animals in connection with the eucharistic meal is shown by a curious incident from the *Acts of Philip*, which belongs to the apocryphal traditions about the apostles in early Christianity. The incident shows how the Eucharist is not only supposed to prevent people from becoming "a natural devouring creature."[9] The *Acts of Philip* probably originate from Encratite circles in Phrygia in modern day central Turkey. Its description of the Eucharist may reflect the practice in the communities there. Mariamne—Philip's sister in the Greek text—prepares flour and salt for the breaking of bread, an activity that the records appear to have counted among the duties of a female deacon.[10] Therefore, a cup of water would have been drunk at the Eucharist.

In chapter 12 of the *Acts of Philip*, two animals present a strange request to the apostle. He had earlier preached the word of God to a leopard and a young goat and baptized them. Following this, they could understand human language and adopted human customs, but they kept their animal form and speech.

After Philip distributed the Eucharist to his fellow apostle Bartholomew and his sister Mariamne, he saw both animals in tears. In response to the apostle's question, the leopard explained to Philip in a well-composed speech, "We were animals without understanding and lived in ignorance until the day when our eyes saw you. I have fed on flesh and blood, and the darkness of the night has been like the light of day to me. As soon as day broke, I would hide myself in the forest. But the moment you came over the mountains, fear and plague came upon us. My animal nature has been tamed and transformed into goodness. I have abstained from eating the kid there because the power of God has come upon us."[11]

The leopard reminds Philip of the various stages of his conversion. The story echoes the biblical motif of peace between animals, the nonviolent coexistence of wild and domestic animals, as promised by Isaiah where the leopard shall lie down with the kid (Isa 11:6–8). With their conversion to Christ, God's peace was now shared between the two animals.

Then the leopard comes to the real concern of the two, "And now we are crying because you have not yet considered us worthy of the Eucharist....We even heard the voice [of the only begotten Son] and we perceived the glory of your petitions and prayers of blessing. If even he counted us worthy to partake in all these miracles, why do you not now count us worthy to receive the Eucharist? That is why we weep and suffer."[12] A theological justification supports the request of the two to receive the Eucharist, "God truly dwells in us....We therefore ask you to accept this miracle of glory from God, who watches over every being, even wild animals, because of his great mercy!"[13] Philip listens to the speech of the leopard and sees the request of the two as a sign that God will visit all created beings through Jesus Christ at his saving return. The apostle confesses, "God cares not only for humans, but also for livestock, and for every living thing."[14]

The leopard and kid apparently receive communion from a chalice of water, just as the Eucharist was practiced by the Encratites. In the process, they undergo another transformation into human beings. Now, the two animals can be there for each other and eat together without one devouring or being devoured by the other. The animals share the food culture of humans in the eucharistic meal.

It would seem I have gotten far away from the question of Jesus and the Eucharist. But according to the Gospel of Mark, the peaceful relationship with nonhuman creatures prompts Jesus to make his first public appearance. In Mark's short version of the temptation, Jesus remains in the desert for forty days. He was exposed day and night to heat and cold in the barren nature; he lived there "with the wild beasts; and the angels waited [*diakonoun*] on him" (Mark 1:13). Mark does not say that Jesus fasted, but Jesus certainly did not use wild animals for food—and there are no domestic animals in the desert. He lives in the original peace between humans and animals, as God intended it to be from the first blessing of creation (Gen 1:29). Jesus holds a meal at which angels are serving him. Table service is a common meaning of the Greek verb *diakoneō*. With angels ministering, it is a holy banquet that Jesus celebrates here, a banquet prepared for him from the vast heavens above the desert. After this desert meal, Jesus begins to proclaim, "The time is fulfilled, and the kingdom of God has come near; repent, and believe in the good news" (Mark 1:15).

In the early Christian period, the Eucharist celebrated more than human communion. It was a celebration of fellowship with God, but also with nonhuman creatures. It is rooted in Jesus's joy in creation. In the next chapter, the Revelation to John brings me to the late period of the New Testament writings, that is, to the 90s of the first century. In Revelation, the meal is also the symbol of the eschatological consummation of all creation.

2

HOW THE RISEN JESUS WANTED THE EUCHARIST

THE BOOK OF REVELATION gives the holy meal imagery that is associated with political resistance. According to this text, the Risen One communicated to John the Seer how he wanted the Eucharist. Eating, drinking, and sharing meals are of great importance in the last book of the Bible.

The Revelation to John is prophetic Scripture written by a Jewish-Christian prophet. He was part of a group or a sort of school that addressed different churches on behalf of God (see Rev 22:9). Prophets received words or visions and proclaimed them in the congregations, speaking in the first person as if the message was a direct communication. In the text, the prophet John often speaks with the "I" of the risen Jesus. He describes prophecies and visionary experiences in his writing with many biblical references and pictures. Many of them are enigmatic but nevertheless striking. His book is the written exegesis of his prophetic experiences, perhaps written down later at a desk on the island of Patmos. His writing was probably sent from the island as a circular letter to seven communities in Asia Minor, from the west coast of modern-day Turkey to the interior of the country.

According to his own testimony, John received the commission to pass on his revelations "on the Lord's day" (Rev 1:10) when he was on Patmos, separated from the churches on the mainland. The mention of the Lord's Day is one of the early pieces of evidence that this day, the first of the week, has replaced the Sabbath as the day for gathering to worship in the Christian congregations. On the island, the Risen One appears to John as "like the Son of Man" (Rev 1:13). The "Son of Man" is a heavenly figure, who, by the time of the New Testament, represented the Jewish hope for the future and the expected replacement of all unjust, inhumane rulers. The head, eyes, feet, and voice of the Risen One are human, yet powerful and assertive (see Rev 1:14–15). The churches to which the Book of Revelation is addressed belonged to the Roman province of Asia. They suffered from the political and military oppression of the imperial power in Rome. Thus, the Risen One who appears to John is not a mythological figure who remains in heaven; he comes and places himself as a human ruler at the side of his faithful.

JESUS KNOCKS AT THE DOOR

At the meal, the Risen One reveals his powerful nearness without becoming overpowering. Jesus himself asks to be let in.[1] He commissions John with seven letters to be given to the churches of Asia Minor. At the end of these letters, he says, "Listen! I am standing at the door, knocking; if you hear my voice and open the door, I will come in to you and eat with you [*deipnēsō*], and you with me" (Rev 3:20).

Jesus stands outside at the door and knocks. He will enter and dine with those who open the door to him. This is reminiscent of a parable of Jesus in the Gospels (see Luke 12:36–38). Jesus gives the disciples an example of servants who are waiting for their master, who is returning from a wedding celebration. Even if his coming is delayed and he knocks late, they should stay awake and be alert (see Luke 12:36). Happy are those who can then open to their master. "Blessed are those slaves whom the master finds alert when he comes; truly I tell you, he will fasten his belt and have them sit down to eat, and he will come and serve them" (Luke 12:37). The parable presumably comes from the oral gospel traditions. At the homecoming meal of the head of the household, the earthly relationships of authority are reversed. The master serves in place of the servants, and the servants take their master's place at the table.

Revelation recasts this parable of Jesus. When the Risen One enters at the table, the change in hierarchical relationships goes even further than in the gospel parable. Dominant relationships have turned into relationships on an equal footing. Being over or under one another has given way to familiar togetherness. The ingathering at the meal is comparable to the lovers in the Song of Songs of the Hebrew Scriptures or in the medieval love poetry, and yet it is different. "I am my beloved's and my beloved is mine," says the beloved in the Song of Songs (6:3). A Middle High German *Minnelied* (love song) says, "Thou art mine, I am thine. Of this thou canst be sure. Thou art locked in mine heart; Lost is the little key: Thou must be therein forever."[2] The lover assures the beloved of his love. She will remain locked in his heart forever. This literally captivating element of love is not present in the meal with the Risen One. The beloved is not trapped in the chamber of her lover's heart, no key is lost. Jesus and the people who open themselves to him become a meal community, but they do not absorb one another, nor do they make demands upon each other. Together they share a meal of freedom without the kind of dominating pressures that Christians faced in their environment.

In the Book of Revelation, this promised meal is followed by a heavenly vision in chapters 4 and 5. It is not the Risen One who enters through the door, but John the author who goes through a door to heaven (Rev 4:1). He is admitted into God's throne room and witnesses the resurrection of Jesus being celebrated in heaven. A slaughtered lamb takes its place by the throne and receives a scroll with seven seals, the heavenly script for the rest of Revelation. It is the book of the history of the world; Holy Scripture, which all can read and understand, is God's word. People will be able to understand every event in history and what God wanted to communicate through it. It is still sealed, but the Lamb will begin to open seal after seal.

Only toward the end of the book does Revelation return to the table fellowship of the beginning. The prophet is given a heavenly commission to write and deliver these words to those who would read and hear the Scriptures. "And the angel said to me, 'Write this: Blessed are those who are invited to the marriage supper [*deipnon*] of the Lamb.' And he said to me, 'These are true words of God.'" (Rev 19:9). The Greek word for meal, *deipnon*, refers to the promised meal at the beginning. What the Risen One promised at the beginning is now being fulfilled; he will have a meal (*deipnēsō*) with those who previously let him and his message into their lives. There is no longer any difference between guest and host. No one must wait on another, and no one is to be served, everyone sits together at the table of the heavenly wedding feast.

A MEAL WITH IMPLICATIONS OF POLITICAL RESISTANCE

Revelation is an impressive testimony of how the gospel message of Jesus was used as a prophetic social criticism toward the end of the first century. The political opponent was an all-powerful Roman state. As the state religion, it demanded unconditional worship of the emperor and his institutions. For Asia Minor, Rome was the protecting power that granted peace. That is why the cities of Asia Minor had joined the imperial cult, spreading it there through an impressive visual propaganda campaign, even before the cult became common in Rome. The imperial power had an enormous presence in the cities that were full of Roman imagery. This is one of the most important explanations as to why Revelation employs its own imagery to help Christians in this situation. It is a counterprophecy to imperial propaganda.

Still, Roman power had its allure. It promised security, it rewarded the people who participated in public banquets and entertainment. The heavenly wedding meal has not yet come for the churches. The Risen One strengthens Christians with this hope in their political resistance. In Revelation, they enter a world of symbols whose heavenly radiance helps them see Roman society and its propaganda differently.

In the center of the heavenly wedding feast stands a lamb. Evil can also take the form of a lamb with two horns (see Rev 13:2, 11). But the Lamb on the throne of heaven bears a clearly visible slaughter wound. Evil is different, evil pretends to be invulnerable. It wants to pretend that there is no suffering, that it can cure any disease. It seduces with seemingly eternally flowing fountains of youth that promise ever-fresh wellness. The Lamb of God, however, can be recognized by its slaughter. It retains the mortal wound inflicted upon it. The Lamb represents the crucified Jesus. Even after the resurrection, Jesus shows his wounds to the disciples; he shows them that he has triumphed while being vulnerable and wounded. In Revelation, the slaughtered Lamb joins the people in the great tribulation and leads them to the meal at the waters of life (see 7:16–17).

How far the meal imagery of Revelation reflects the meal practices in the congregations is disputed. In his three-volume commentary on Revelation, David E. Aune makes the Scriptures understandable in their historical situation with a wealth of biblical and extrabiblical sources. Regarding the question of the meal in the congregations, he writes, "In a Christian context, it is natural to think of the meal as the Lord's Supper, at which the risen Jesus was thought spiritually present (see Luke 24:30–31)," and he explains, "Sharing food was perhaps the most common way of establishing a sacred bond between individuals and between individuals and their deities."[3] Certainly therefore, Revelation, like no other book of the Bible, shaped the development of the Eucharist and liturgy.

MEAL AND PRAISE

The meal of the Lamb is accompanied by the praise of all creation, which has already begun in heaven. Whoever opens the door to the Risen One on earth to dine with him enters this heavenly praise. Like John, whoever enters takes part in the heavenly celebration of the resurrection of the lamb that was slain. The seer described the praise of God in heaven that he saw in his vision:

> In front of the throne there is something like a sea of glass, like crystal. Around the throne, and

> on each side of the throne, are four living creatures, full of eyes in front and behind: the first living creature like a lion, the second living creature like an ox, the third living creature with a face like a human face, and the fourth living creature like a flying eagle. And the four living creatures, each of them with six wings, are full of eyes all around and inside. Day and night without ceasing they sing,
>
> "Holy, holy, holy,
> the Lord God the Almighty,
> who was and is and is to come." (Rev 4:6–8)

The four living creatures are originally from the opening vision of the prophet Ezekiel (see Ezek 1:5–25), and their song of praise is the same Thrice Holy as the seraphim from the Book of Isaiah, also from the prophet's commissioning vision (see Isa 6:3). The Thrice Holy was already part of Jewish liturgies in New Testament times and was known as the *Kedushah*. From there it found its way into Christian liturgies. References to the four living creatures are also part of the liturgy and church architecture. In the tympanum of the central portal of Chartres Cathedral, the four living creatures surround the Risen One, who appears in his glory. The imagery of the grand doorway prepares those entering for what awaits them inside the church during the liturgy. In the sanctuary, the congregation hears the word of God, which is proclaimed from Christ's heavenly throne through the four Gospels. Since the time of the church father Irenaeus of Lyon (c. 130–c. 202), these four creatures have been interpreted as the four Gospels, usually in the same order as in Ezekiel: the angel (or human) represents Matthew, the lion is

Mark, the bull is Luke, and the eagle is John (see Ezek 1:10). They are to reach all four corners of the world from which the four winds come. This interpretation has become part of the tradition of the Western Church.

For John himself, though, it is more likely that the four beasts originally represent all of creation before God's throne. They are part of the heavenly realm that already gives glory to God. John's order is also different from that of Ezekiel. Each represents a different type of creature in creation before the heavenly throne: the lion represents untamed, wild land animals; the bull or ox represents tamed, domestic animals; the eagle represents birds; and the human-faced creature represents human beings. As symbolic representations of every type of living creature, they stand in amazement before God's throne. They are covered in eyes, symbolizing that they remain awake to praise God without ceasing. Their praise, which starts in the inner circle of the heavenly throng, begins to spread in the first vision. Hosts of other angels join them and finally every creature in heaven, on earth, under the earth, and in the sea joins the four living creatures in heavenly praise for the victory of the slain Lamb (Rev 5:11–13).

THE *SANCTUS*

The Thrice Holy, which the four living creatures offer, and which was already known in the Jewish liturgy as the *Kedushah*, matches the *Sanctus* in the liturgical meals of the Christian churches. Jewish and early Christian sources reemphasize and expand the seraphim's praise of God from Isaiah, especially the second half. Isaiah renders the hymn, "Holy, holy, holy is the LORD of hosts; / the whole earth is full of his glory" (Isa 6:3). Later changes and expansions adapted the *Kedushah* to specific literary or liturgical contexts. The

Sanctus in the Liturgy of the Eucharist represents such an expansion of this tradition. With the addition, "Blessed is he who comes in the name of the Lord, Hosanna in the highest,"[4] the congregation prepares for a twofold coming—that of Christ in the Eucharist and his eschatological coming into the world.

In Revelation, the second line is also changed in the praise of the four living creatures. Instead of "the whole earth is full of his glory," the living beings praise God "who was and is and is to come" (Rev 4:8). This does not suggest a negative view of material, nonhuman creation; rather, John sees creation consumed and destroyed by the forces of evil. The damaged creation is therefore no longer able to reflect God's glory. It has been subjected by those "who destroy the earth" (Rev 11:18). Revelation describes in frightening visions how Christians experienced the damage to earth. These visions show how a consumer society consumes itself through wars, military occupations, famines, greed, and death. Earthly and unearthly powers have dominated with their destructive powers, but the global threat will come to an end when all the inhabitants of the earth will again fear God and acknowledge God as their Creator (Rev 14:7).

Thus, the *Kedushah* in Revelation 4 contains a statement about the eschatological future. God is praised as the one who is to come. This is not only a statement about God's nature, but also God's coming to creation. It means judgment as well as salvation: judgment on those who destroy the earth, and the salvation of the earth from their hands.

At the end, when God invites creation to the meal, the now-rescued creation will praise God. *All* living beings are to praise God. Among them, human beings are just one of God's creatures like other animals. Humans are not singled out—even in the description of the four living beings, humans are only mentioned third. Biblical theology affirms that all creation praises God. Even nonhuman creation praises God simply by existing. In the renewed creation, the original community between human beings and other living beings is restored. Psalm 104 counts mountains, springs, wild animals, asses, birds, cattle, people, trees, cedars, lions, and even the devouring sea monster, Leviathan, as part of the renewed creation. Then, it says,

> These all look to you
> to give them their food in due season;
> when you give to them, they gather it up;
> when you open your hand, they are filled with
> good things. (Ps 104:27–28)

All creation awaits God's coming because all creation receives life, sustenance, and salvation from God.

HOW DID THE RISEN JESUS WANT THE EUCHARIST?

In Revelation, the comforting images of the meal are surrounded by images of cruelty; complex monsters, dragons, violent beasts, pale horsemen, bloodthirsty beings, and flashy, filth-filled, false prophets who are carefully covered with gold and glamour, purple and pomp. Christians are to resist the hegemonic mechanisms taking hold of the earth and defy the opulence of the palaces of luxury that rise amid widespread poverty. When the congregations of the Book of Revelation celebrated a meal together, it was a meal whose peace and freedom were threatened on all sides.

The Risen One reveals a theological interpretation of the meal to John; it is the heavenly wedding meal, which, presumably, was anticipated in the congregational meal. In the meal, heaven and earth celebrate together and people experience their connection with God's resurrected creation. God gives them what they eat, the fruit of the tree of life (Rev 2:7; 22:2), and "the hidden manna" (Rev 2:17). People no longer have to kill and slaughter for their meals. Like the birds, wild beasts, and tame animals, human beings are called to the heavenly throne to praise God.

It is hard to recognize official roles within the community in Revelation. That does not necessarily mean that they did not exist, but they were not allowed to impair the collaborative community of believers with the Risen One. Overall, nothing can be inferred from Revelation about offices, regulated procedures, forms, or communal prayers at the meal celebration. The next chapter goes into a very different text, though, the church order known as the *Didache*. With its appeal to apostolic provenance, it claims to give "the Lord's teaching" on the celebration of the meal.

3

THE ORIGIN OF THE PRAYERS OVER THE OFFERINGS

THE EUCHARIST IN THE *DIDACHE*

THE *DIDACHE* PROBABLY originated in southern Syria, since there is a distinct similarity in many places between this text and the Gospel of Matthew, which also likely originated there. Matthew reports that people in Syria had heard Jesus at the beginning of his public ministry (Matt 4:24). This is probably an attempt to project the birth of the then-present Syrian messianic congregations back to the early days of Jesus's ministry. The *Didache* provides a common church order for Christians in these congregations. Its liturgical sections include instructions for baptism and the celebration of the Eucharist.

The full Greek title of this text is *Teaching of the Twelve Apostles*, but it is known as the *Didache* for short, from the Greek word for "teaching." Its title claims apostolic authority for itself, but probably none of the apostles was alive at the time the book was written. However, their authority was widely recognized throughout the Church by the end of the first century. Thus, from this point in time, writings appeared more frequently under their names. This development can also be observed in the New Testament Gospels. While the older Gospels according to Mark and Luke were still distributed under the names of "colaborers" of the Twelve, the Gospels according to Matthew and John[1] were already ascribed to apostles. The later gospels, which were not included in the New Testament, only bear the names of apostles: Thomas, Philip, Peter, and so on.

The *Didache* is the oldest surviving Christian church order. It is dated around AD 100 and is thus the earliest evidence that the celebration of the meal is called "thanksgiving" (*eucharistia*). In addition to the "Eucharist," the celebration of the meal is also called the "breaking of bread" in the *Didache* (14:1). According to the Acts of the Apostles, the term "breaking of bread" (*klasis tou artou*) is even older than *eucharistia* because that is what the meal that the followers of Jesus ate in their houses in Jerusalem after Pentecost is called (Acts 2:41). The celebration got its name from two essential moments of the ritual meal: the prayer of thanksgiving and the breaking of the bread, which is then distributed among the participants. The *Didache* preserves the oldest prayers of thanksgiving at the eucharistic meal of a Christian community.

The congregation celebrated their thanksgiving on "Lord's day" (*kyriakē*—the root of our word "church") (*Did.* 14:1). As in the Book of Revelation, the day of their celebration is no longer the Sabbath, but the day after the Sabbath. On Lord's Day, the congregations gathered at the meal to celebrate their communion with the risen Christ. Like in the Book of Revelation, prophets would visit the congregations as itinerant charismatics. Prophets were allowed to speak in the congregations publicly at the meal and recite freely formulated eucharistic prayers. It is quite possible that women also spoke as prophets. In the Acts of the Apostles (21:9) four daughters of Philip are named as prophets and there were also women who spoke as prophets in the church meetings (see 1 Cor 11:5; Acts 2:17; Rev 2:20; also, Anna in Luke 2:36).

Unlike in the Book of Revelation, the words of the prophets in the *Didache* relate to practical questions in the community, such as how the agape meal should be held, and which needy members of the community should be given a meal (*Did.* 11:9). In addition, *episkopoi* and *diakonoi* were elected from the congregation for various ministries.[2] It is uncertain what these ministries were. Settling disputes or managing the congregation's finances may have been part of them, possibly also presiding over the celebration of the Eucharist; but nothing is expressly stated.

The *Didache* contains the Our Father from the Gospel of Matthew. As it is the Lord's Prayer, it should be prayed three times a day. It is found just before the instructions for the Eucharist. Eckhard Nordhofen has argued on several occasions that the petition for bread in the Lord's Prayer was related early on to the eucharistic bread.[3] At the Eucharist, the congregation asks for "bread for tomorrow, for all the future, for the time after that, when the tent is struck down again after 33 years (as per the life of Jesus)."[4] The placement of the Lord's Prayer in the *Didache* is a possible first indication of such an understanding. However, the section can also be understood as an order for daily prayer.

THE PRAYERS OVER THE OFFERINGS OF WINE AND BREAD

According to the *Didache*, the Eucharist was a full meal. Wine was drunk and bread was eaten. Liturgical prayers framed the eating and drinking. The fact that everyone was satisfied at the meal can be gathered from the introduction to the prayer of thanksgiving after the meal: "After you are filled, thus give thanks" (*Did.* 10:1). Even if it is not expressly stated for the meal, the ethics of the *Teaching of the Twelve Apostles* make it clear that the social differences at the church meal should not determine what and how much someone gets to eat. Thus, it is written in the parenetic passages before the description of the Eucharist, "Give to every one that asks you, and ask it not back; for the Father wills that to all should be given of our own blessings (free gifts).... Woe to him that receives; for if one having need receives, he is guiltless; but he that receives not having need, shall pay the penalty, why he received and for what" (*Did.* 1:5).

The *Didache* still shows the original connection between the term "eucharist" and prayers of thanksgiving. The section on the celebration of the Eucharist begins with the words, "Concerning the Thanksgiving [*peri de tēs eucharistias*], thus give thanks [*houtō eucharistēsate*]" (*Did.* 9:1).

Strikingly, the sequence of prayers does not begin with a prayer over the bread, as in Paul's tradition of Jesus's Last Supper in the First Letter to the Corinthians, but with praise over the cup: "We thank you, our Father, for the holy vine of David your servant, which you made known to us through Jesus your servant" (*Did.* 9:2). Only then does the blessing over the broken bread follow: "We thank You, our Father, for the life and knowledge which You made known to us through Jesus Your Servant" (*Did.* 9:3).

After the satisfying meal, a concluding prayer of thanksgiving is said, as was customary at the Jewish meal: "We thank You, holy Father, for Your holy name which You caused to tabernacle in our hearts, and for the knowledge and faith and immortality, which You made known to us through Jesus Your Servant" (1 Cor 10:2). The congregation answers each of the three prayers of blessing with "To You be the glory forever!"

In the bread and wine, the community of the meal gives thanks to God for Jesus, who is the prophetic messenger sent by God to reveal God to God's people. Just as eating and drinking physically strengthens the members of the congregation, so God made God's name known through God's ambassador Jesus and let it dwell in the hearts of those who ate. God's life has entered the cycles of human eating and drinking. The prayer recalls the "deepest dream that culture has achieved, of having God absorbed and incorporated in the same way that bread is digested by a human being."[5]

BROUGHT TOGETHER FROM THE ENDS OF THE EARTH

The prayer over the offerings and the prayer of thanksgiving are supplemented by additional prayers that explain the meaning of the meal even more precisely. In these, the congregation gives thanks that God is gathering them into this meal as God's people at the end of time.

God gathers Israel, who has been scattered among many different peoples. This is one of the main themes of the biblical writings after the Babylonian exile. In their work on the Hebrew Scriptures and New Testament, Norbert and Gerhard Lohfink have shown that Jesus also understood his mission as a gathering of Israel. Since the great conquests, first of the Northern Kingdom of Israel by the kingdom of Assyria in 722 BC, then of the Southern Kingdom by the kingdom of Babylon in 597 with the fall of Jerusalem in 587, large parts of the upper class and the entire population were deported. Since then, Jews have lived scattered in the diaspora, not only in countries far to the north of Israel, but also in the south, in Egypt, in Jewish diaspora communities up the Nile. Only a remnant of the people remained in the country. However, the biblical prophets had kept alive the expectation that God would gather the dispersed Jewish people together again and lead them back to the promised land. When Israel returns to its land, the other nations will also come and join themselves to it. They will be taught the Torah by God along with Israel so that they can end their alienation and war. Then, God will grant them a great banquet on the hill of the city of Jerusalem.

The biblical expectation that God would gather his people was familiar to the communities of the *Didache*. Therefore, the supplementary eucharistic prayers of the *Didache* call the church *ekklêsia*, a Greek word which originally means assembly. The prayer of thanksgiving after the meal says, "Remember, Lord, Your Church [*ekklêsia*], to deliver it from all evil and to make it perfect in Your love, and gather it together from the four winds, sanctified for Your kingdom which You have prepared for it" (*Did.* 10:5).

Having shared a meal together, the congregation sees itself as part of God's great gathering of God's people Israel. The four winds should not bring heat, drought, or floods over the earth to damage land, sea, and trees. They should bring together the scattered people from the four cardinal directions to unite them again into one people. An additional prayer about the broken bread says, "Even as this broken bread was scattered over the hills, and was gathered together and became one, so let Your Church [*ekklêsia*] be gathered together from the ends of the earth into Your kingdom" (*Did.* 9.4).

The imagery of this prayer combines the various processes needed for the community to be able to share bread among themselves at the meal: the grain was sown in the fields ("the hills"), collected at harvest, ground, and baked into bread as flour. In the congregational gathering it was torn up as flatbread and distributed so that everyone received a chunk of the bread. At the meal, *one* piece of bread was probably broken and given to the revelers. In this symbolic gesture, they were able to experience the gathering through their senses. Paul also speaks of the *one* bread of the Eucharist (1 Cor 10:17): *The meal community becomes what it eats. It acquires an overall sacramental quality. It becomes a part of the eschatological congregation of God's people.*

THE EUCHARIST AS PASCHAL CONTINUATION OF JESUS'S MEAL PRACTICE

Jesus also saw himself as part of this eschatological gathering movement. He saw his work as being closely connected to that of an eschatological ambassador, whom the Jews of his time expected to come as "the Son of Man." Jesus says that the Son of Man will come with a loud trumpet and send out his messengers to gather "his elect from the four winds, from one end of heaven to the other" (Matt 24:30–31 // Mark 13:26–27).

In Luke 13:34 (// Matt 23:37), Jesus speaks of gathering the people together. He speaks in the name of the Wisdom of God. In the Hebrew Scriptures and in Judaism at the time of Jesus, the Wisdom of God is personified as a woman; like the Son of Man, she is a heavenly figure standing next to God. The Son of Man was expected to be a figure that God would use to bring a human society to God's oppressed and tormented elect. Lady Wisdom, however, has accompanied both God and humans since creation. From the beginning, she has taught people the fear of God. Jesus sees his work as one with Wisdom;[6] therefore, Jesus speaks as one of the prophets, as if he was speaking for them himself: "Jerusalem, Jerusalem, the city that kills the prophets and stones those who are sent to it! How often have I desire to gather your children together as a hen gathers her brood under her wings, and you were not willing" (Matt 23:37).

The inhabitants of Jerusalem are to be gathered to form the center of the eschatological congregation of people. But they rejected and killed the prophets and messengers who were sent before and after Jesus. The city and its people refused, yet nevertheless God chose them for his banquet meal of the peoples at the end of time. In doing so, Jesus takes up a widespread motif in the Hebrew Scriptures—the accusation against his own people—and combines it with an image of his own work that bears very maternal traits. As a mother bird entices and protects her young and warms her nest with her wings, so Jesus, the Wisdom of God, gathers his people.

Matthew and Luke found the lamentation about Jerusalem in a source of Jesus's sayings that predates the two Gospels and is no longer extant. Lohfink suspects that the cry of lamentation over Jerusalem comes from the later period of Jesus's ministry.[7] In the Gospel of Matthew this saying is found in Jesus's last eschatological speech in Jerusalem, as is the saying about the coming of the Son of Man (see Matt 23:37–38).

In this saying, too, Jesus speaks in the first person as Wisdom personified. "Eating wisdom" is a colloquialism in German, for example, in the idiom that someone has "eaten wisdom with a spoon."[8] In the biblical and early Jewish idiom, accepting wisdom is often expressed metaphorically as drinking or eating. Those who have digested the Wisdom of God can put an end to the earthly need to eat or die.

In the Book of Proverbs, a biblical wisdom book, Wisdom is also a woman. She invites others to a festive holy meal; tables are set, cattle are slaughtered, and wine is mixed. Lady Wisdom sends out her maids to gather her guests. From the top of the town citadel, they proclaim their invitation to the meal in all directions. When the guests arrive, Lady Wisdom opens the meal,

> Come, eat [*phagete*] of my bread
> and drink [*piete*] of the wine I have mixed.
> Lay aside immaturity, and live,
> and walk in the way of insight. (Prov 9:5–6)

Here, eating and drinking represent an internalization of the knowledge and fear of God, which is the beginning of wisdom. More precisely, this is the greatest possible physical acquisition of wisdom. It is quite possible that the "eating and drinking of Wisdom" was present at the meal with Jesus, even at the Last Supper. At this meal, the image of eating and drinking is ritualized. Only in the Gospel of Matthew does Jesus expressly ask his disciples to eat and drink at the Last Supper. He does this while passing the bread and handing the cup. When he says to his disciples, "Take, eat [*phagete*]" and "drink [*piete*] from it, all of you" (Matt 26:26, 27) he uses the same verbs as Lady Wisdom in her meal invitation. The Evangelist Matthew thus draws a line back to the beginning of Jesus's public ministry. In the Beatitudes at the beginning of the Sermon on the Mount, his first discourse, Jesus says, "Blessed are those who hunger and thirst after righteousness, for they will be filled" (Matt 5:6). Whoever eats of the bread and drinks from the wine that he gives out enters into a physical relationship with Jesus. This changes the person's life, who then becomes a part of Jesus's gathering movement. When the *Didache* refers to the biblical idea of gathering in its meal prayers, it allows the congregations to continue Jesus's message and meal practice from Easter.

THE PRAYERS OVER THE OFFERINGS IN THE CATHOLIC LITURGY OF THE EUCHARIST

The modern Catholic Liturgy of the Eucharist replaces the *Didache*'s eucharistic prayers with the prayer over the offering. In this prayer, the celebrant gives thanks for the bread and wine, just as the presiding officer of the celebration did in the eucharistic prayers of the *Didache*. The liturgical reform after the Second Vatican Council gave a new form to these prayers and the preparation of gifts. Unfortunately, so far little theological reflection upon this new form of the celebration has made much impact. When the offerings are brought to the altar after the Liturgy of the Word, two prayers are said over the bread and wine. Over the bread, the priest says, "Blessed are you, Lord God of all creation, for through your goodness we have received the bread we offer you: fruit of the earth and of work of human hands, it will become the bread of life for us." Similarly, over the cup, "...for through your goodness we have received the wine we offer you: fruit of the vine and work of human hands." The congregation affirms the praise over bread and wine each with the cry, "Blessed be God forever."

The models for these two prayers were not the prayers of the *Didache*, but rather Jewish meal prayers. According to rabbinical testimonies, at Jewish meals each guest at the head table praised God the Creator over their own cup of wine: "Blessed are You, Adonai our God, King of the universe, who creates the fruit of the vine." The guests each offered this prayer themselves because they did not yet have a congregational table. This prayer only occurred once the diners had sat down at the table in the dining room. There, the host then blessed the bread and praised God: "Blessed be Adonai our God, the king of the world, who brings forth bread from the earth." As a sign of approval, the guests responded with "Amen"—"so be it!" whereupon the host distributed the bread among them.

The prayers over the offerings as they are said in the revised celebration of the Eucharist reveal the model of these Jewish prayers, but they also make their own biblical references. When the bread is brought to the altar, the celebrant asks for it to become "the bread of life." This expression comes from the passage in John 6:51, "I am the living bread that came down from heaven." Thomas Ruster has drawn attention to a twofold relationship to the manna in the desert and to Jesus's self-sacrifice in his life and death.[9] Jesus announces his surrender in the same verse (6:51): "The bread that I will give for the life of the world is my flesh." Jesus is the bread of heaven. Israel received this bread in the desert from God and not from Moses. Now Jesus gives himself as this bread. Ruster comments, "Self-*surrender* instead of self-assertion."[10] Jesus becomes the bread of life. Through this, God breaks into the human cycle of taking and giving. At the meal with Jesus, God gives without asking for anything in return. Humans cannot give this divine food; not even a great man like Moses can do so, because when people give, they tend to expect something in return. But this also means that no human institution nor church can claim sole power over this food. The bread from heaven is a gift freely given: God's precious communion for those who accept it.

The prayer of blessing over the chalice also contains a biblical allusion: The chalice is to become the "chalice of salvation," according to the German and older English translations. However, this is an imprecise translation of the original Latin prayer because there the chalice is called *potus spiritalis*—a "spiritual drink."[11] Paul used this expression to remind the church in Corinth of the exodus and the subsequent procession through the desert: "All ate the same spiritual food, and all drank the same spiritual drink" (1 Cor 10:3–4a). Bread and wine thus allow Christians to participate in Israel's exodus experience. For Paul, Christ is a "spiritual rock" (1 Cor 10:4b) who was already accompanying Israel during the exodus.

With prayers of blessing over the offerings, the celebrant asks on behalf of the congregation that God feed them with the gifts that have nourished Israel on the way to the promised land. The church shares a fellowship with God's people, Israel.

NO MORE VICTIM?

The liturgical reforms following Vatican II used these two prayers to replace a sequence of medieval prayers said by the priest alone, traditionally called the *offertorium* ("sacrifice"). Opponents of the liturgical reform saw this as meaning that the sacrificial character of the Mass had been lost through the revision of the preparation of the gifts. The

Didache, which preserves the earliest tradition for the form of these prayers of thanksgiving, is also the oldest writing in which the Eucharist is called a sacrifice: "Every Lord's day gather yourselves together, and break bread, and give thanksgiving after having confessed your transgressions, that your sacrifice may be pure. But let no one who is at variance with his fellow come together with you, until they be reconciled, that your sacrifice may not be profaned" (*Did.* 14:1–2).

The eucharistic meal is clearly to be celebrated peacefully here. "Pure" and "profaned" refer here to this interpersonal meaning. It is unclear what is meant by "your sacrifice"; possibly thanksgiving prayers as a bloodless sacrifice in contrast to the bloody sacrifices in other temples, the celebration of the Eucharist as a whole, or the eucharistic gifts of bread and wine.[12] In my opinion, the similarity to a saying of Jesus in Matthew's Sermon on the Mount speaks in favor of the last interpretation: "So when you are offering your gift at the altar, if you remember that your brother or sister has something against you, leave your gift there before the altar and go; first be reconciled to your brother or sister, and then come and offer your gift" (Matt 5:23–24).

Jesus originally meant that people should be reconciled on the way to the temple in Jerusalem. The fact that participation in the temple cult requires people to live together peacefully corresponds to biblical and Jewish tradition (see Ps 15:2–4). However, by the time the Gospel of Matthew began circulating, the temple no longer existed. In the Christian congregations where it was read, the sacrificial offerings most likely were related to the offerings that were eaten together at the eucharistic meal. Eating the bread and drinking the wine should bring the congregation together, and that could not happen if they remained at odds during the celebration. In the *Didache*, the sacrifice could also refer to the bread and wine that Christians brought to the Eucharist.

In the prayers over the gifts in today's eucharistic celebration it is said that the gifts are "offered" to God. In the Latin version this is clearer. In German, the prayer reads, "we bring this (bread/chalice) in your presence" (*Wir bringen dieses Brot / diesen Kelch vor dein Angesicht*). In Latin, it reads, *quem tibi offerimus* ("which we offer to you"—the English translation is more faithful to the Latin). However, even in the German version, the biblical language of sacrifice still resonates. Sacrifice, in the Bible, does not mean that something is destroyed before God, let alone violently by God. Sacrifice is not about some particularly painful renunciation. Rather, sacrifice means something that is brought before God, and usually for a joyful occasion. Sacrifice regularly leads to a banquet, to which God is summoned as a "guest of honor"[13] with gifts and fragrant perfumes.

Therefore, characterizing the Eucharist as a meal does not diminish its sacrificial character, as is often claimed. In the Torah, in the oldest law—the Book of the Covenant which was revealed to Israel on Sinai after the Exodus narrative—the showbread is commanded as such a sacrificial meal: "You shall set the bread of the Presence on the table before me always" (Exod 25:30). With the showbread, God is offered a "holy banquet" that people then eat together. The sacrificial meal of showbread can already be understood as a *sacrum convivium*, as Thomas Aquinas describes the Eucharist.[14] In the sacrificial meal, the people of Israel celebrate their *convivium*, their living in communion with God. While eating and drinking, the people assure themselves through all their senses of God's blessing and presence. God also includes the congregation that celebrates the Eucharist together in God's covenant with God's people Israel.

God does not need sacrificial food:

> If I were hungry, I would not tell you,
> for the world and all that is in it is mine.
> Do I eat the flesh of bulls,
> or drink the blood of goats? (Ps 50:12–13)

Bachl remarks, "This sounds like the comment of one who is fed up with the infinite perfection of one's life. But it is precisely because of the freedom of God's power that God can participate in the sacrificial feasts that are held for God in order to allow blessings to go from that point into the human world."[15]

NO SACRIFICING ILL-GOTTEN GOODS!

Through the prayers over the bread and wine during the preparation of the gifts, the congregation gives thanks to God for creation. The Argentinian philosopher Enrique Dussel has repeatedly pointed out that the bread and wine in the Eucharist come not only from creation, but also from the economic processes of production.[16] Religious liturgy is bound by references to economic processes. Wine can be adulterated to increase profits. At the end of a long supply chain, bread can be purchased, although people who are often at the beginning of those chains are denied a fair wage. Dussel has described the economic processes that flow into the celebration of the Eucharist as a "circle of production." It begins with (1) a person as the subject in need. Through (2) work, the person makes the (3) land, the earth, fertile. From this, the person obtains (4) bread and other crops, which the person then consumes again to maintain his or her (5) life. A person depends on food throughout her or his life, and so again identifies her as a (1) needy subject:[17]

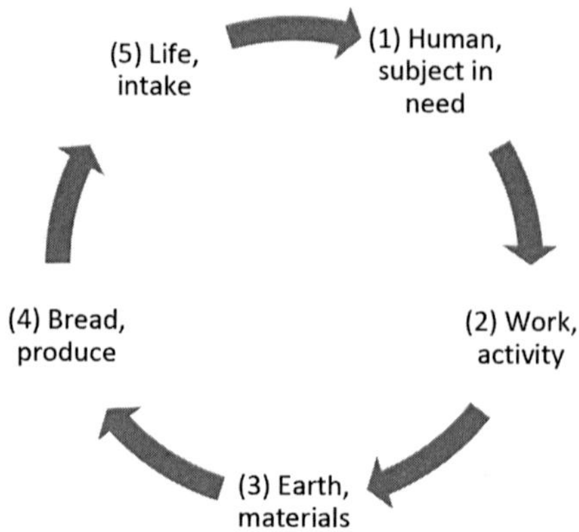

Bread and wine and the interpersonal economic relationships and processes that produce them are included in the gift-giving in God's economy—in God's administration of all of creation. God enters the productive cycles of economic economy with God's blessing for humans and nature. Dussel recalls Bartolomé de las Casas who, in 1514, refused to celebrate the Eucharist with the *conquistadores* because he did not consider the bread that had been unjustly confiscated from the natives to be worthy of celebrating the Eucharist with. "He began to think that the misery and slave labor under which these (indigenous) people suffered was unjust and tyrannical."[18]

A saying in the wisdom book Sirach underscores the close relationship between worship and economic activity in the preparation of the gifts, which caused Las Casas to change his mind. It demands that the gifts offered in the temple come from just economic conditions.

> If one sacrifices ill-gotten goods, the offering is
> blemished;
> the gifts of the lawless are not acceptable.
> The Most High is not pleased with the offerings of
> the ungodly,
> nor for a multitude of sacrifices does he forgive
> sins.
> Like one who kills a son before his father's eyes
> is the person who offers a sacrifice from the
> property of the poor.
> The bread of the needy is the life of the poor;
> whoever deprives them of it is a murderer.
> To take away a neighbor's living is to commit
> murder;
> to deprive an employee of wages is to shed
> blood. (Sir 34:21–27)

Jesus ben Sirach wrote in the second century BC and was a tutor for upper-class youth in Jerusalem. The sacrificial business in the temple was a present reality to him and his disciples. The wise teacher understands the spotless sacrifice that the Torah prescribes (Lev 22:18–25) on the horizon of social justice. The poor are especially dear to God. Exploiting them is a grave sin against God's justice and mercy. Sirach underscores this with a drastic comparison: Whoever offers a sacrifice that comes from the possessions of the poor offers a son as a sacrifice in front of his own father.

The massive experiences of sexualized violence in the churches today require renewed theological reflection and sensitivity in order to speak of the Eucharist as a sacrifice.

Speaking of the plight of many Christians, a survivor says, "I am waiting for the liturgy to be cleansed of misleading notions about sacrifice." All too often the Eucharist is associated with false understandings of the concepts of sacrificial death: God wanted to reconcile people with themselves through the death of his Son as atonement. The biblical ethic of sacrifice, evident in Sirach, is a clear objection to such theological misunderstandings. For a son to be sacrificed in front of his father is the worst thing that this wise teacher could imagine happening in Israel. That could never be a gift pleasing to God. Only a gift that comes from righteous and humane action can be offered as a sacrifice pleasing to God.

INCIDENTALLY...

Calling the celebration of the Eucharist "the Sacrifice of the Mass" can easily be misunderstood and should therefore be avoided. Linguistically, three concepts can be distinguished from the single word "victim" (*Opfer*), which, however, often flow together when the word is used in German. In English, "victim" refers to a living being who is intentionally or unintentionally killed. This includes victims of accidents and violence. A "sacrifice" is distinguished from this; a sacrifice is when part of one's produce—whether crops or livestock, but always precious—is offered for religious reasons. This is the sense in which the congregation offers its gifts of bread and wine in the Eucharist. Finally, the term can also refer to the *voluntary surrender* that a person makes for a specific end. In extreme cases, this can mean one's own life. The New Testament understood the death of Jesus as a voluntary surrender (see John 10:11, 15, 18). In the celebration of the Eucharist, the congregation commemorates this surrender; it is a memorial of Jesus giving his life *and* his salvation from death. *The prayers over the offerings commemorate the devotion of Jesus and recall the exodus. They ask God to be near, so that the revelers in the congregation who eat and drink the gifts together can be there for one another and for others.*

4

THE LAST SUPPER

THE *DIDACHE* DOES not mention Jesus's words of institution for the celebration of the Eucharist, whether from the First Letter to the Corinthians or from any other tradition of the Last Supper. In general, the *Didache* makes no reference to the body and blood of Jesus in the celebration. It cannot be said with certainty whether the meal was followed by further eating and drinking, which then would have given a stronger symbolic and ritualized element to the congregations' Eucharist.[1] The *Didache* congregations likely knew the tradition of Jesus's Last Supper from one of the Gospels, probably Matthew, including the words about bread and wine.

The oldest tradition of Jesus's Last Supper comes from Paul in the First Letter to the Corinthians, written around the mid-50s. The congregation's meal was already called the "Lord's Supper" (*kyriakon deipnon*, 1 Cor 11:20). This designation does not come from Paul himself, because he reproaches the congregation in Corinth that their celebration is no longer a "Lord's Supper." It was probably also celebrated on a Sunday (1 Cor 16:2) as in the congregations of the *Didache* and Revelation.

We have seen that the day of their meetings is already called "Lord's Day" there. *The meal granted communion with the risen "Lord" Jesus. This meal actually belonged to him. Even the hosts who housed the church at this meal were guests at the Risen One; it was not meant to be their private meal.* Eating and drinking together should anticipate something of God's just, peaceful, and joyful world.[2] Paul criticizes the believers in Christ in Corinth that they see it as their "own supper" (1 Cor 11:21).

A double celebration at Corinth is sometimes assumed based on later testimonies. A main meal was held first and then afterward a sacramental meal at which the tradition of the Lord's Supper was then also proclaimed. However, it is only in the third century AD that there is explicit documentation that the words of Jesus at the Last Supper were also spoken in the liturgy as *verba institutionis* (words of institution).[3] In the *Traditio Apostolica*, the "Apostles' tradition," an aforementioned church order in the Roman context, the words of initiation belong to a longer prayer at the Eucharist for episcopal consecration.[4] In the postconciliar liturgical reform, this prayer was the inspiration for the newly created second Eucharistic Prayer. However, the history of transmission of this writing is complex, and the Eucharistic Prayer with the words of institution is not included in the entire transmitted text there either. For Corinth, there is no reliable evidence that the words of Jesus at the Last Supper were recited in a separate part of the celebration. This assumption often presupposes an overemphasis on the words of institution. In the case of Paul, Jesus's Last Supper is above all an ethical model for the congregation's meal.

PAUL AND MARK

Paul is harsh regarding the way the meal was held in Corinth. The Corinthians' "Lord's Supper" no longer corresponds to the event they are celebrating. Paul uncovers the problem there: "Each of you goes ahead with your own supper" (1 Cor 11:21). Perhaps some understood the celebration as a Greek *eranos* meal. At these sumptuous friendship meals, all the guests brought something with them and made it available for commoners.[5] By then, they would then have eaten some of what they had brought with them on the way or helped themselves generously from their own bags at the meal. Perhaps some of them met beforehand for a private meal, which only later became the celebration of the meal with the rite of bread and cup.[6] The exact circumstances are difficult to determine, but the culture of a holy meal had been lost here. Each person reached out their hand as quickly as possible before others could. Paul's advice to the Corinthians is very biblical: "Wait for one another" (1 Cor 11:33). This recalls Psalm 104:27–28, speaking of all creation: "These all look to you / to give them their food in due season." To wait for one another, to have one's own food handed to one by another, and to regard the other as the one who gives one the food in due season—that is dining culture. This certainly applies to the holy meal but goes beyond it as well.

If this conflict had not existed, the oldest tradition of Jesus's last supper would not have come down to us. In their dispute over the meal, Paul reminds the Corinthian congregation of Jesus's supper,

> For I received from the Lord what I also handed on to you, that the Lord Jesus on the night when he was betrayed took a loaf of bread, and when he had given thanks, he broke it and said, "This is my body that is for you. Do this in remembrance of me." In the same way he took the cup also, after supper, saying, "This cup is the new covenant

> in my blood. Do this, as often as you drink it, in remembrance of me." For as often as you eat this bread and drink the cup, you proclaim the Lord's death until he comes. (1 Cor 11:23–26)

Paul himself had already received as church tradition what he passes on to Corinth. The tradition of the Last Supper in Paul has several similarities to the tradition of Jesus's last supper, as it is found later in the Gospel of Mark toward the end of the 60s but there are also some differences. The most important thing they have in common is that Jesus bound the bread and wine at the supper to the explanation,

> While they were eating, he took a loaf of bread, and after blessing it he broke it, gave it to them, and said, "Take; this is my body." Then he took a cup, and after giving thanks he gave it to them, and all of them drank from it. He said to them, "This is my blood of the covenant, which is poured out for many. Truly I tell you, I will never again drink of the fruit of the vine until that day when I drink it new in the kingdom of God." (Mark 14:22–25)

In Paul's account, the course of Jesus's last supper can be roughly divided into three parts: (1) Jesus opens the supper with a prayer of blessing and provides the gesture of sharing the bread with a saying of interpretation; (2) this is followed in the middle by the actual meal; and (3) "after the meal" Jesus concludes the common meal with a word of blessing over a chalice and hands it around with another explanation.

This process could also have corresponded to the meal in the church in Corinth, except that a host or possibly also a hostess[7] took over the role of Jesus as the head of the meal.

The tradition of Jesus's Last Supper does not say what happened after the cup of blessing. From the context of 1 Corinthians, it is probable that the congregation's meal did not end there, but that the celebration of the meal was followed by a type of "Liturgy of the Word." At a Greek symposium, the sequence of meals and social gatherings with talks was followed by witty stories, music, and speeches. The congregation in Corinth would then have adopted it for a religious communal meal where the supper was followed by Psalms, teachings, prophecy, and utterances in unknown languages with their translation for the "building up" (1 Cor 14:26) of the church.[8]

It is striking that Paul's tradition of the Lord's Supper does not speak of "wine" but of the "chalice." It could therefore have been mixed wine or even just water in the chalice. In fact, as we have seen, beverages other than wine were used at the Lord's Supper in the early centuries. In Mark, on the other hand, it is implicitly assumed in 14:25 that Jesus drank wine with his disciples. As they drink wine now, so wine will be drunk in God's new world.

The sequence of events in Mark's tradition of the Lord's Supper also differs slightly from that in 1 Corinthians, but it is still recognizable. While the symbolic actions over the bread and wine correspond to those in Paul's account, in Mark, Jesus takes the bread only after the meal has already been going on for a while. Jesus's prayer of blessing over the bread does not open the meal in Mark as it does with Paul. Here, the bread and cup follow one another directly; there is no meal in between. Another difference is that Jesus says the interpretation of the cup only after the disciples have drunk from it. After drinking together, Jesus can interpret this as a covenant community with which he awaits the kingdom of God.

MATTHEW AND LUKE

The two oldest versions of the Lord's Supper discussed above were models for the two other, later versions that are also found in the New Testament: Luke and Matthew. The situation with Luke is complicated because the Lord's Supper was transmitted in two different versions in the early manuscripts of his Gospel; some manuscripts contain a longer version and others a shorter version. I will return to the shorter one later. As a rule, modern Bible translations only reproduce the longer version. This provides a connection with Paul and Mark. Therefore, in Luke, a cup of wine is drunk twice with an accompanying saying from Jesus. By doubling the cup, the bread is at the center of the meal. Jesus's command is only found with the bread: "Do this in remembrance of me." In Paul's tradition of the Lord's Supper, this command occurs twice, once after the bread (1 Cor 11:23) and again after the cup (1 Cor 11:25).

The Evangelist Matthew adopted Mark's version. His most striking addition is that Jesus speaks of the "forgiveness of sins" at the cup: "This is my blood of the covenant, which is poured out for many *for the forgiveness of sins*" (Matt 26:28). With this, Matthew has added one of his own important themes to the words over the cup. The cup that the disciples drink fulfills what Jesus taught them to pray for both in the Lord's Prayer and in the Sermon on the Mount (Matt 6:12a). Matthew associates God's promise not only with death, but also with the name of Jesus which conquers the forces and powers of injustice and people's sins. "He will save his people from their sins," is how the angel interprets the name of Jesus to Joseph before his birth (Matt 1:21). At the Last Supper, this becomes particularly clear in the person of Judas. Luise Schottroff drew attention to the social pressure of Rome and the conformist Jerusalem ruling elite, from which Judas could not escape: "Judas's deed shows how a person becomes entangled in the social pressure of Rome and his wrong can no longer be undone. He took part in the Last Supper. He too was forgiven for his sins (Matt 26:28) as Jesus promised to the fellowship."[9]

These observations show that there was no single wording for the tradition of the Lord's Supper that all were bound to. This was a living tradition in the early days and could be adapted to different situations and interpretations. Even the version of the *Traditio Apostolica* from the beginning of the third century, which states that Jesus's words of institution should be recited in the service, does not correspond exactly to any of the New Testament versions. Schottroff reflects a widespread research consensus when she writes, "[Nor can] a meaning which is valid for the later church be ascribed to Paul's earliest version. The term 'words of institution' already presupposes an institutionalization of the church and of the Lord's Supper. It is misleading to use it for New Testament times."[10]

A PROPHETIC, SYMBOLIC ACTION

Rudolf Bultmann assumed that the meal tradition of Mark 14:22–25 was a "cult legend for the specifically Hellenistic celebration [of the Lord's Supper] from the Pauline sphere"[11] that had been included in the Gospel. This view persists widely today, that the depiction of the Lord's Supper in the New Testament is a cult tradition for the celebration of the community, or even a cult etiology—a founding narrative for the celebration. Clearly, the congregations attempted to make Jesus's Last Supper present at their meal celebrations based on Paul and Luke's inclusion of Jesus's commission to celebrate the meal in memory of him. This did not refer to the words that Jesus spoke about the bread and wine; the remembrance was not just about Jesus's martyrdom and his death, but about his entire life and actions. Through his resurrection, "a new future has come…their hands, feet and lives now belong to the Messiah because they are the body of Christ."[12]

In Mark and Matthew's depictions of the Last Supper, Jesus does not give any such commemorative commission, but even in these Gospels, the listeners must have recognized the meal celebration of their own congregation when hearing these words. In the Gospel according to Mark, this association is heightened by the fact that Jesus has his disciples prepare a Passover meal, but then the story does not tell of a Passover meal, with its celebration of several courses, but of a simple meal with bread and wine. The change of perspective in the narrative of this meal made it possible to recognize the Christian communal meal. Nevertheless, the communion traditions are not cult legends. They are integrated into the overall narrative of the Gospels. It is likely too, for Paul, that the tradition of the Lord's Supper was also part of a more comprehensive tradition of the death and resurrection of Jesus.

At the Lord's Supper, Jesus performed a symbolic action similar to those of prophets in the Hebrew Scriptures. Symbolic actions by prophets were provocative: Ezekiel bakes barley cakes on cattle manure and drinks a few sips of water. He thus announces that the people of Jerusalem will weigh their bread and measure water with worry. The people of Jerusalem will be unclean and eat their bread among the nations (Ezek 4:9–16). In another sign, Ezekiel shaves his beard and hair with a sharp sword. He burns a third of it in the city, scatters a third to the wind, and hides the last part in the tail of his robe. "This is Jerusalem," God says through him (Ezek 5:5). A short prophecy, like Jesus spoke over the bread, "This is my body." The disciples would have understood this. In the Bible, the body means one's whole person (see Ps 63:2; 84:3). *When Jesus tears up the bread and distributes it, they understood that what happens to the bread will happen to himself.* Shortly before, a woman had anointed Jesus at the supper, and Jesus interpreted her anointing as a prophetic foreshadowing of his death (see Mark 14:3–8). This too, then, was a prophetic symbolic action.

However, Jesus's sign with the bread goes even deeper than the anointing of the woman. He himself tears the bread and gives it to his disciples to eat, indicating his own willingness to accept violent death. Paul is still aware of this meaning when he writes to the Corinthians that they announce the death of Jesus with the supper: "For as often as you eat this bread and drink the cup, you proclaim the Lord's death until he comes" (1 Cor 11:26). In the renewed, post–Vatican II liturgy, this is incorporated in a call to the congregation to respond to the tradition of the Last Supper: "We proclaim your death, O Lord, and profess your resurrection until you come again." However, for Paul, the coming of the Lord is also the coming of judgment, which he warns the congregation about since they are misusing the meal to mark social differences instead of solidarity.[13]

The shorter of the two versions of the Lord's Supper tradition in Luke's Gospel is very close to the original prophetic testimony of Jesus. The Passover meal that Jesus longed for with his disciples begins with a cup of wine. According to rabbinical testimonies about the Jewish Passover meal, this corresponds to the kiddush cup that is accompanied by blessings during the first dish. With this cup, Jesus announces that after this meal he will no longer drink of the fruit of the vine until he does it again with his disciples in the kingdom of God. Jesus then takes the bread, from which he tears off a piece for each of his disciples, to point to his coming death. The second saying over the chalice is missing in the short version. Immediately after the saying over the bread, which is still shorter than that of the long version, Jesus makes prophetic reference to one of his table companions, who will hand him over to the court. Judas is not mentioned by name:

> When the hour came, he took his place at the table, and the apostles with him. He said to them, "I have eagerly desired to eat this Passover with you before I suffer; for I tell you, I will not eat it until it is fulfilled in the kingdom of God." Then he took a cup, and after giving thanks he said, "Take this and divide it among yourselves; for I tell you that from now on I will not drink of the fruit of the vine until the kingdom of God comes." Then he took a loaf of bread, and when he had given thanks, he broke it and gave it to them, saying, "This is my body, which is given for you. Do this in remembrance of me." And he did the same with the cup after supper, saying, "This cup that is poured out for you is the new covenant in my blood. But see, the one who betrays me is with me, and his hand is on the table." (Luke 22:14–21)

With the sign and words about the bread, Jesus predicts his death. With his words about the wine, he speaks of his confidence. The Last Supper is not an end. Jesus enters the cycle of human consumption, but his life will not be counted as loss. He will continue to celebrate with his disciples when the kingdom of God comes. He will drink wine, because wine not only nourishes the stomach like bread, wine gladdens the heart (Ps 104:5), and wine not only gives joy to people, but also to gods and angels (Judg 9:13).

As a prophetic symbolic action, Jesus's gestures and words about bread and wine were open to interpretation. In the bread that was distributed, the disciples could not only recognize his death, but also that he gave himself to them in this bread. Not only was the bread torn and divided, but it satisfied their hunger like the manna in the desert and restored strength to their bodies. Therefore, they could understand the bread as a symbol for everything that Jesus's incarnation meant for them. In the wine, they could remember the joy that Jesus had in eating together with tax collectors and sinners.

5

THE FIRST EUCHARISTIC CELEBRATION AT EMMAUS

"BREAKING BREAD" IS the oldest description of the common meal and Luke refers to it in this way. Luke's double work—the Gospel and the Acts of the Apostles—as a relatively late writing in the New Testament, surveys approximately forty to fifty years of the history of the Eucharist. Luke attempts to integrate the different stages in his Gospel and in Acts. In doing so, he provides insights into the origin and history as well the theological significance of the first Christian celebrations of the meal.

The Gospel of Luke preserves a tradition that the celebration of the Eucharist began *after* the resurrection of Jesus. Luke concentrates this historical memory in his account of the disciples at Emmaus (see Luke 24:13–35). Later ecclesiastical tradition often depicts the Evangelist as an iconographer. Historically, however, there is nothing to suggest this, except that Luke is a masterful storyteller; his stories have become something like *narrative* icons. The story of the Emmaus disciples is one of them. It is one of the most moving stories in the Bible.

Two disciples are wandering along the way. Luke later mentions the name of one of the two, Cleopas, but he does not name the other. Women had returned from Jesus's tomb early on the first day of the week and reported finding the tomb empty. Shortly thereafter the two disciples must have left. They are on their way to Emmaus, about sixty stadia from Jerusalem—about a two-hour journey. The Risen One joins them, but "their eyes were kept from recognizing him" (Luke 24:16). They think he is one of the many foreign pilgrims to the festival returning home, just not with their same disappointment. He seems unaware of the situation and when he asks them about their disappointment, their faces fall (literally, "looking sad" [Luke 24:17]). Luke tells the reader from the beginning that the one who the disciples thinks is a stranger is actually Jesus (see Luke 24:15), but the disciples don't realize it. The tension in this story comes from the different levels of knowledge about the identity of the stranger between the two disciples and the readers.

As the pair advance along the way, so too does the day. The disciples have a long chat with the supposed stranger. Meanwhile, evening has begun to fall, and they still have not recognized him. At last, they invite him to their place so that he does not have to go on alone in the falling darkness. They finally recognize him at the meal. When he was talking to them on the way about the Messiah and expounding the Scriptures, he was talking about himself all the time. Only when their eyes open at the meal do they notice how their hearts were burning on the road with Jesus.

The eyes of the two disciples open when Jesus breaks bread for them. "When he was at the table with them, he took bread, blessed and broke it, and gave it to them" (Luke

24:30). The sign of Jesus here is the breaking of bread. The Risen One is the guest of the pair, but he acts as a Jewish host. Jesus had already broken bread for them at the Last Supper, but it is only now, after the resurrection, that Luke's breaking of bread acquires its full meaning. The gesture makes the meaning of Jesus's life sensible to both disciples. When they eat the bread, they get more than just nourishment for their bodies that will get hungry again. They notice what makes their hearts burn. They eat to live—and to have life abundantly, as Jesus put it. Only the Risen One can communicate his new life in abundance to the disciples through the bread.

"Breaking bread" occurs only in a few places in the Hebrew Scriptures and only in connection with a funeral meal. The prophet Jeremiah prophesied regarding the hardship of Jerusalem's conquest that there would be no more funeral meals for relatives, "No one shall break bread for the mourner, to offer comfort for the dead; nor shall anyone give them the cup of consolation to drink for their fathers or their mothers" (Jer 16:7).[1] At the meal of the Emmaus disciples, the sorrowful circumstances of Jeremiah's prophecy of doom are reversed. Jesus shows himself to them as alive after his death and eats with them. His breaking of bread irrevocably reverses their grief. When they return to Jerusalem, they also see the city in a new light. The meal with the Risen One thus becomes the pivot point between Jesus's meal practice in the previous Gospel and a preview of the meal practice to follow in the Acts of the Apostles.

MARY AND CLEOPAS

Christian Herwartz, SJ, founded the spiritual movement "Retreats on the Street" (*Exerzitien auf der Straße*). In this form of the *Spiritual Exercises*, one does not retreat to the seclusion of a church building, but meditates on everyday life on the streets and in the places of the big city, in department stores, on squares, in front of prisons.[2] On the retreats, Herwartz kept coming back to the story of the street conversation between the Risen One and the Emmaus disciples and discovered something about it that the scholarly exegesis of the text has so far barely noticed:

> Although Jesus valued both men and women, they [the women] are missing; their names are often left out of New Testament narratives—in accordance with social custom—or they are even replaced by male ones. Jesus accepted the testimony of a Canaanite woman and healed her daughter; he also learned from another woman who washed his feet with her tears...and did the same in his own difficult situation. Therefore, it would not be surprising if the second person who left for Emmaus was also a woman. While searching for her name, I discovered three women standing under the cross at the hour of Jesus's death. All three are called Mary. Among them, John names the second person, Mary, the wife of Clopas (John 19:25). Could Clopas and Cleopas refer the same person?[3]

Christian Herwartz identifies the nameless disciple in the pair as a woman: Mary, the wife of Clopas. The two "disciples" were a couple. After all that had happened, they were looking for a private place outside of the circle of the apostles.

> On the road to Emmaus, a stranger (Luke 24:17) asks the "disciples" what they are talking about.—

> Cleopas brusquely rejects him and, asserting his masculinity, protects the intimacy he has fought for with the rhetorical question, "Are you the only stranger in Jerusalem who does not know the things that have taken place there in these days?" (Lk 24:18). The fellow traveler asks again, "What things?" (Luke 24:19–24). Now Mary and Cleopas both answer and together they tell of their sorrow and the hope they found for themselves and their people through the life and message of Jesus. When a husband and a wife talk about reality together, the statements become more vivid because they combine different points of view. This makes it easier for them to get to the heart of the matter.[4]

It is only when they both tell the story that Jesus opens their eyes to what Scripture says about the Messiah: "And their hearts burned with joy (Luke 24:32), now that they understand the reality of the prophetic statements."[5]

An icon of the couple can be seen in the Benedictine monastery of Nütschau in northern Germany. Ansgar Stukenborg, OSB, has rewritten the icon of the Emmaus story, showing Mary and Clopas inviting Jesus in as he enters. When Jesus breaks the bread, Mary opens her arms in amazement and Clopas points to the Risen One with a look of understanding.

As an Aside...

The two who were on their way to Emmaus are commonly called "disciples." However, Luke himself does not use the corresponding Greek expression in this narrative. He writes that "two of them" set out, and by "them," he means a larger circle of women and men who mourned the death of Jesus in Jerusalem. He often calls this circle "disciples." "Student" would be another possible translation of the Greek word (*mathētēs*) that Luke uses. In the New Testament, the masculine form of "disciples" (*Jünger*) or "students" (*Schüler*) can often be an accurate translation in gendered languages like German because in several New Testament texts, the Gospel of Matthew, for example, women are not included. Among the followers of Jesus, Luke also distinguishes "apostles" from the larger group of disciples. With very few exceptions (Acts 14:4, 14), Luke always means the circle of the twelve apostles. For others, such as Paul, "apostles" can also refer, in a broader sense, to messengers and authorized persons who came forward with a commission from Jesus or the congregations; women were also counted among the "apostles" in this broader sense. The twelve whom Luke calls the apostles establish a connection between the community of followers of Jesus and the twelve tribes of Israel. They represent the people whom Jesus saw as his mission to gather. As twelve men, like the twelve sons of Jacob, they represent eschatological Israel; they represent a larger group of women and men. Several generations, living and dead, are represented here. According to Luke, Matthew, and Mark, the Twelve celebrated the Lord's Supper with Jesus. That is why the Catholic Church sees the foundation for the ecclesiastical office in the twelve apostles. The fact that the twelve apostles were men and that the disciples are often referred to with masculine words does not in itself preclude the fact that official roles related to the Church's celebration of the Eucharist were also exercised by women. Why should the church make gender the sole criterion for the office of the apostles and disciples of Jesus, but not their religious origin, since they were all Jewish? In the New Testament environment, representation in public space was largely exercised by men. That has changed fundamentally since then.

AN EXEMPLARY NARRATIVE

The English New Testament scholar Richard Bauckham has shown on philological and historical grounds that it was probably Mary, as a disciple, who was traveling with her husband Clopas on the way to Emmaus.[6] John calls her "Mary the wife of Clopas" (John 19:25). Cleopas is the name of one of the two "disciples" on the way to Emmaus in Luke (see Luke 24:18). Cleopas is the short form of the Greek name Cleopatros and is not the same as the Semitic name *Qlôpa'*. However, it could easily be used as a Greek equivalent, for Jews during this period often adopted Greek names that sounded similar to their original Semitic ones. The two were a married couple who probably spread the gospel in Jewish Palestine. Married couples were missionaries together more often during the time when the gospel was first spreading. Since men and women lived very different experiences from one another in New Testament times, it was easier for a married couple to win both women and men to the gospel.

It is disputed to what extent Luke is drawing upon older traditions in the Emmaus narrative. Most scholars believe the story to be legendary as Luke adhered to the literary forms of the Hellenistic historiography of his time. He did not compile historical facts but made history comprehensible as a narrative. Events, speeches, and backgrounds were designed in such a way that they made the progression of the story flow better. Luke often does this by using examples. He masterfully reworked the Emmaus story and told it with great skill. If it is not entirely unhistorical, Luke may have incorporated a memory that the Risen One appeared to Clopas. His name may have been remembered in the first congregations, and as Herwartz reminds us, the names of the women and others who were there have not been preserved because that was the custom of the time. Why should it be impossible for the risen Jesus to appear together to the couple or to their entire household?

However, Luke has probably reworked another historical memory into this story: *the Eucharist began after Easter at various places as meals at which the disciples experienced Jesus as the Risen and Living One, and in such a way that they remembered his past life, death, and resurrection in his presence.*

THE MEAL OF THE PENTECOST COMMUNITY

According to the Pentecost narrative in the Acts of the Apostles, more than three thousand people accepted Peter's word and were baptized.[7] The new trust in God and in the community finds expression in the communal breaking of bread. The believers sealed this trust and their acceptance of the proclamation of the risen Messiah Jesus through baptism. The communal identity of the crowd is first established not through the meal, but through baptism in the name of Jesus Christ. Speaking of the great Pentecostal assembly, Luke writes,

> They devoted themselves to the apostles' teaching and fellowship, to the *breaking of bread* and the prayers. Awe came upon everyone, because many wonders and signs were being done by the apostles. All who believed *were together* and had all things in common; they would sell their posses-

> sions and goods and distribute the proceeds to all, as any had need. Day by day, as they spent much time together in the temple, *they broke bread at home* and [all] *ate their food* [together] *with glad and generous hearts*, praising God and having the goodwill of all the people. And day by day the Lord added to their number those who were being saved. (Acts 2:42–47, italics and bracketed words added)

The breaking of bread is mentioned twice here, and it is embedded in a broader communal ethic. The description of the first church is often viewed as a utopian idealization. However, it reveals a widespread communal ethos. The common ownership among this great multitude follows the ethical values of Greek friendship. Even more important than collective ownership, however, is that the wealthy supported those who were in need with their possessions. The rich were actually willing to give up their private property. Likewise, at the meal in their houses, the poor and hungry got enough to eat: the baptized shared the food among themselves, which is the meaning of the corresponding Greek formulation in verse 46. Breaking bread meant the food and drink was there to share so that no one went hungry or remained thirsty.

CONNECTING THE MEAL TO THE HOUSE CONGREGATION

The shift of religious practice from the temple to household communities had already begun in Judaism *before* Jesus. According to Luke, however, this was a decisive step in the development of early Christianity: the first congregation in Jerusalem has the group of twelve for its hierarchical center. It moves between worship in the temple and prayer meetings in individual homes. On the other hand, in Paul's missionary proclamation, the connection to the temple is severed from the time when the congregations take in Gentile believers. From then on, the house became the basic religious community. In the environment of early Christianity, the house was not a private sphere, but stood for many interconnected social relationships in which individuals lived with family, servants, and enslaved people. In the house, people experienced dependency and/or exercised authority, in the house they developed their self-confidence and their view of the world, and in the relationships of the house community, self-confidence and worldviews were tested daily. For the Christian celebration of the Eucharist, this social space became the house of God. This development became irreversible no later than AD 70, when the imperial Roman legions destroyed the temple in Jerusalem, and it is already apparent in the Acts of the Apostles.

The Roman centurion Cornelius receives the Spirit of God with his house at the meal, whereupon Peter cannot help but accept the entire non-Jewish household into the community of believers (Acts 10:44–48; 11:3). Lydia, a merchant of purple goods, urges Paul and his companions to have a meal at her home after crossing the Hellespont from Asia Minor to Macedonia (Acts 16:14–15). The midnight meal that the jailer at Philippi feeds Paul and Silas in his house is the sign that he has come to faith (Acts 16:34). The boundary between a eucharistic liturgical meal and a nonliturgical meal is often not clearly defined. At another meal in Troas, Paul resurrects Eutychus, a young man who fell asleep during his sermon and fell out of a third-story window. This is perhaps a rather amusing event today, but for the early Christians, sleepiness and death were images of their past lives. For Luke, this event tells of the saving power of the celebration of the meal. The narrative begins, "On the first day of the week, when we met to break bread..." (Acts 20:7). The breaking of bread is here a fixed term for the liturgical celebration. Unlike the breaking of bread in the Pentecost narrative, here it is specified *who* breaks the bread. After Paul resurrects the boy, Paul breaks the bread (Acts 20:11). The celebration continues in an agape feast with a lengthy conversation until dawn. Thus when Paul breaks the bread, as the Risen One did, he also conveys the life-giving power of this meal.

The Second Vatican Council renewed the Eucharist in the Catholic Church in such a way that the celebration could again be experienced as a liturgical meal in a community. Joseph Ratzinger, for example, welcomed this in an early essay in the 1960s: "The altar table used to be recessed and one could almost get the impression that it was mainly just the base on which the tabernacle stood; the high altar stood...far away from the faithful—just as a king keeps an appropriate distance from his visitors. Today the altar has moved away from the wall and has moved closer to believers again, who often group around it in a semicircle, with the altar in the center. Again, what the altar actually is emerges: a table on which the faithful celebrate Christ's Last Supper, the commemoration of the sacrifice(s) on the cross."[8] The Eucharist celebrates more than just the memorial of the sacrifice of the cross though. The New Testament attests that Jesus Christ, with the power of his resurrection gives his blessing and presence to the celebrating congregation.

Conclusion

FINDING A WAY FORWARD

A DIVERSE COMMUNITY AROUND THE LORD'S TABLE

PROTESTANT CHURCH historian Hans Lietzmann distinguished between two different basic forms in the early Christian development of the Eucharist and this distinction remains important today.[1] The first form corresponds to the *Didache*'s celebration of thanksgiving for Jesus with bread and wine and has no institution narrative. This pattern includes a Syriac eucharistic liturgy of Addai and Mari (who, according to tradition, were two disciples of the apostle Thomas in Edessa) from the second or early third century. It also has no words of institution and was recognized by the Roman Congregation for the Doctrine of the Faith in 2001. According to Lietzmann, this basic form goes back to the open meal practice of Jesus himself. The second basic form corresponds to the meal in Corinth as a commemoration of death with an institution narrative. The *Traditio Apostolica* from the beginning of the third century, for example, preserves this form. This second form would have been shaped by Christian missionary congregations with the cult legend of Jesus's Last Supper, as Gentile Christians took part in the meal.

Along this journey, we have seen an abundance of forms and interpretations of the celebration of the Eucharist even in the early days of the writings of the New Testament. This diversity expanded in the first centuries before it was subject to stronger standardization later. *The documented variety of celebrations resists dividing the early Christian liturgies into two basic forms with two different foundational impulses.* Historically, according to Luke's double work, the following explanation is more likely: What Luke writes about Emmaus and Jerusalem was exemplary for different places where followers of Jesus came together. From the experience of a living relationship with the risen Jesus, they began to celebrate together in remembrance of Jesus's life and death. The common ground of their celebrations was their belief in the resurrection of Jesus. In the proclamation of the resurrection of Jesus, Paul also saw the common message that he, despite many differences, shared with everyone else: "Whether then it was I or they, so we proclaim and so you have come to believe" (1 Cor 15:11).

The variability and variety of the sacred meal in the first Christian congregations does not reveal any final and complete form of the celebration of the Eucharist. Dorothea Sattler and Volker Leppin's ecumenical study group has concluded that "we will have to dismiss the idea that there is only one way in which to celebrate the fullness of what Jesus Christ founded. This means, however, that one can recognize and acknowledge elements in other traditions that are not contained in one's own."[2] The various manifestations of the celebration cannot be harmonized into a single form even based on their origins in the early church. The initial foundation of Jesus, the testimony of the New Testament, and apostolic tradition have authentically taken shape today in various denominational forms of the celebration. Their diversity therefore contains elements of complementarity and encourages us to recognize that the ecclesial celebration of the Eucharist has been authentically preserved in the other forms as well. *The various celebrations of the sacrament of the Eucharist and the Lord's Supper have their unity through their common focus on the coming Jerusalem. They are always a sacred meal along the journey, which did not end at Emmaus for the pair of disciples on the road either but led them on the same evening to Jerusalem—and united them with the other disciples. In the coming Jerusalem, God will gather God's people and will then feed them in the eschatological meal.*

PROPHETIC SPEECH

It is difficult to determine from the New Testament and early Christian sources who led the first eucharistic celebrations. The ecumenical study group has summarized this finding: "We know little about the leadership of the first congregational meals, even though Paul lists leading worship services among the charisms (1 Cor 12:28; see also 1 Thess 5:12–13; Rom 12:8). Because charisms are gifts of God without regard to gender or position, it can be assumed that in the first generations of the Church (see Rom 16:1), and even beyond this time in part at least, women held leadership positions (see Acts 16:14–40)."[3]

While the question of leadership is hardly the focus of the New Testament sources, another charism can be inferred from them: prophetic speaking. This gift was significant for the celebration of the Eucharist from the beginning. It was through eating and drinking together that the Christian house churches experienced God's presence among them with the gifts of God's Spirit. God's Spirit was active when God's word was opened to them in public prophecy. Early on, if not from the beginning, male and female prophets had the task of influencing the arrangement of the meal and of interpreting it. Their prophetic words were not based solely on inspiration or intuition. Attention to the everyday experiences along with the study of the Scriptures and of the tradition of Jesus were equally important impulses for their public speeches in God's name. According to Acts, the words of male and female prophets were part of the first Christian communal ethics. In his sermon at Pentecost, Peter sees the promise in the Book of Joel being put into effect,

> Your sons and your daughters shall prophesy,
> and your young men shall see visions,
> and your old men shall dream dreams. (Acts 2:17;
> see Joel 3:1–5)

In today's Catholic liturgy, the place for a public prophetic word is the homily. It can still reach and change the hearts of hearers, and frequently, even when the preacher's intention is not what gets through. However, this is often prevented by church regulations that exclude women and others from preaching. Laypeople only get the floor for this central preaching in exceptional cases. Barbara and Michael Mertes call this an ecclesiastical "emergency stop-gap principle." If necessary, where there is no longer a priest or deacon, laypeople may undertake the preaching. Regarding ecclesial participation of the laity in pastoral care and liturgy, Mertes and Mertes have stated generally, "Many lay people would be willing to take on pastoral and liturgical tasks… if they were only allowed [and] encouraged to do so….The decisive encouragement would consist of a clear rejection of the stop-gap principle, or to put it positively, in developing such services into 'proper' offices."[4] The early Christian testimonies about the Eucharist present a clear mandate to the church to reorganize the offices and tasks in the sacrament of the meal.

FOOD AND DRINK

In the first Christian congregations, the sacred meal consisted of eating and drinking as a community. It was only after the time of the New Testament that the sacramental meal became more and more distant from everyday eating and drinking. The bread became the host whose shape is no longer reminiscent of daily food, but of the moon or the sun. This development brought new forms of piety to light. Seeing the host and chalice raised at the consecration and venerating them became more important than consuming them. This prayerful gaze at the host enabled an intimate relationship of communion similar to what the risen Jesus says of the meal in Revelation. The Risen One promises to those who let him in, "I will come in to you and eat with you, and you with me" (Rev 3:20). These words are not unlike those of a man in a story of John Vianney. The pastor of Ars found the man staring at the tabernacle and asked him what he was doing. The man replied, "I look at Jesus and he looks at me."

However, if the relation of the celebration of the Eucharist to eating and drinking is lost, it is missing an important aspect from its beginning. There are communities and congregations that bake the bread for the eucharistic celebration themselves. It is then included in the activities of everyday life. In areas where it is possible, the wine can also come from the vineyards of members. The bakers and vintners join in the celebration as their work is blessed in the eucharistic meal. However, it is just as important that the sacrament of the meal also emanates a blessing for everyday eating and drinking. The "Jesus Meal" (Bachl's phrase) points to God who in goodness feeds everything that lives (see Ps 145:15). "The inedible breaks into edibility, the holy and useless into the network of functional usefulness."[5] The sacramental meal makes us aware that eating is more than supplying the human body with new fuel. Factory farming, industrial agriculture, genetically modified seeds, and fields overfertilized to maximum capacity are the result of global food chains. The food that is put on the table has become farther and farther removed from the people who planted, grew, and harvested it. The shelves of the supermarket chains are usually well stocked, yet still what is left for the poor, as in Jesus's parable, is literally what falls from the tables.

From its origins, the Christian table sacrament was not a luxury meal. Jesus and the first congregations expected mouth-watering eating and drinking in the coming Jerusalem. There "the LORD of hosts will make for all peoples a feast of rich food, a feast of well-aged wine" (Isa 25:6). God will give this abundance, and all the world will rejoice over it.[6] The Christian celebration of the meal anticipated this joy, not in the abundance of food, but through the experience of communion. The bread that the early congregations shared at the sacred meal was the same bread that they ate in their kitchens and the same bread that those who were starving in the streets lacked.[7] Thus, from the beginning, congregations had official roles that looked after the needs of the poor or made sure that the poor did not go hungry during the meal. When Christian congregations today ask for bread in the Lord's Prayer in their liturgies, they combine their longing for heavenly bread[8] with the cry of the poor for earthly bread, and for many other things that they lack. The celebration of the Eucharist and Lord's Supper with their prayers do not replace a sustainable global food program. However, they can support Christians in advocating for socially and ecologically responsible sustenance.

FROM THE HOUSES TO THE WORLD

According to Acts, the celebration of the Eucharist in the community of Pentecost began with the baptized gathering in their homes and breaking bread among themselves with joy and sincerity of heart. A renewal of the Eucharist can come from being together in homes today when neighbors and friends gather. The homeless, the lonely, those with sorrow, or those with joy can be guests. With a prayer, the bread and wine can be blessed, and the Risen One can be welcomed as a guest at the meal. Eating and drinking together defies grief and death and gives life new strength. Thus, the meal becomes a celebration of the resurrection by which God conquered death. Protestant and Catholic Christians can already share a meal in their homes. People who are no longer interested in church and such celebrations can be there. With sensitive mutual respect, interreligious hospitality may even be possible. This would not be a common celebration of the Eucharist and no shared Lord's Supper, but Jesus's promise would still apply: "For where two or three are gathered in my name, I am there among them" (Matt 18:20). Ecumenical understanding between churches can grow organically in such celebrations, so that theological objections might no longer inhibit unity.

The last meal in Acts takes place on a large ship, which could be compared to a twentieth-century ocean liner, designed for both freight and passengers. Paul is to be taken to Rome as a prisoner (Acts 27). Other prisoners, sailors, and passengers are with him for a total of 276 men—a motley group of travelers from different countries. South of Crete, the ship gets caught in a heavy storm and drifts rudderless through the sea for several days. Onboard, they lose heart, stop eating, and face their deaths. After fourteen nights, Paul encourages them once again at dawn and tells them to eat from their remaining supplies. As he speaks, he takes a piece of bread, thanks God in front of everyone, breaks the bread, and begins to eat (Acts 27:35). It takes a while, but then the others take courage and everyone on the ship eats together. In the end, all 276 travelers are saved. When Paul breaks the bread, he joins a community of people in need. By eating and drinking together, they defend themselves against despair and death.

The meal on the ship is a picture of God's eschatological salvation. Magdalene Frettlöh earlier noted that eating together opens community across borders, divisions, and graves. Women and men, children and elderly, prisoners, beggars, strangers, and friends are all part of it. The multitude of those who have been saved cannot fit within the walls of an earthly house or within the walls of a church building. Neither can the city limits of Jerusalem nor any other earthly city contain them, nor even any earthly country, for God wants to give this salvation to all peoples. The Eucharist is an anticipatory meal of saved humanity. This is how the risen Jesus wanted it. It defies death, and Jesus breaks bread for the despairing on their way into God's world of justice.

NOTES

INTRODUCTION

1. "Ecumenical Church Day" is a meeting of lay German Protestants and Catholics. Hundreds of thousands of people attended the first two *Ökumenischen Kirchentage* during Pentecost of 2003 and 2010. The third ecumenical congress took place in Frankfurt am Main from May 13–16, 2021.

2. Volker Leppin and Dorothea Sattler, eds., *Gemeinsam am Tisch des Herrn / Together at the Lord's Table* (Freiburg im Breisgau: Herder, 2020). This is the title of the volume produced by the ecumenical study group.

3. The Gospel of John differs significantly from the other gospels in its presentation of the Eucharist. For example, it has no institution words at the Last Supper. If Jesus "instituted" anything on this occasion, it was for his disciples to wash one another's feet, which was a sign of hospitality, but was done only by slaves or very intimate companions. I hardly go into the Gospel of John in the following essay because its position on the Eucharist is very controversial. For the washing of the feet, see Michael Theobald, *Eucharistie als Quelle sozialen Handelns: Eine biblisch-frühkirchliche Besinnung* (Göttingen: Vandenhoeck & Ruprecht, 2007), 24–62.

4. The three-volume documentation of the international and domestic Sacred Meals Project is a valuable contribution. David Hellholm and Dieter Sänger, eds., *The Eucharist: Its Origins and Contexts; Sacred Meal, Communal Meal, Table Fellowship*

in Late Antiquity, Early Judaism, and Early Christianity (Tübingen: Mohr Siebeck, 2017). There, reference is made to almost all other important literature.

5. Gottfried Bachl, *Eucharistie: Macht und Lust des Verzehrens* (Sankt Ottilien: ESO Verlag, 2008), 60.

6. Luke 7:33–34; Matt 11:18–19b; cf. James Kelhoffer, "John the Baptist as an Abstainer from Table Fellowship and Jesus as a 'Glutton': (Non-)Participation in Meals as a Means for Gaining Social Capital That Can Conform or Jeopardize a Person's Standing in Society (Luke 7:31–35 // Matt 11:16–19)," in *Old Testament, Early Judaism, New Testament*, vol. 1 of *The Eucharist: Its Origins and Contexts: Sacred Meal, Communal Meal, Table Fellowship in Late Antiquity, Early Judaism, and Early Christianity*, ed. David Hellholm and Dieter Sänger (Tübingen: Mohr Siebeck, 2017), 313–29.

7. Bachl, *Eucharistie*, 60.

8. *Liturgischer Wegweiser durch de Gottesdienst in de EKHN*, Theologisches Seminar der EKHN (Frankfurt am Main: Zentrum Verkündigung der EKHN, 2018), 31.

9. AC. 7.1 (German). The same article of the *Confessio Augustana* also states, "Nor is it necessary that human traditions, that is, rites or ceremonies, instituted by men, should be everywhere alike. As Paul says, 'One faith, one baptism, one God and Father of us all" (Eph 4:5–6). The diversity of eucharistic celebrations in the early Christian period, which is yet to be shown, reinforces the message of this Reformation text.

10. *Liturgischer Wegweiser*, 53.

11. Lutheran liturgies also use an epiclesis. The liturgical guide of the Evangelical Church in Hesse and Nassau reads, "Therefore we ask, sanctify us with your presence. Send your Holy Spirit on bread and wine. Let us recognize in them Jesus Christ and feel the power of renewal" (*Liturgischer Wegweiser*, 56–57). While the noun for spirit in German and Latin is masculine (*Geist*, *spiritus*) and in Greek (*pneuma*) neuter, in the Hebrew Bible the word for spirit, *ruach*, is overwhelmingly feminine.

CHAPTER 1

1. Gottfried Bachl, *Eucharistie: Macht und Lust des Verzehrens* (Sankt Ottilien: ESO Verlag, 2008), 157.

2. Andrew B. McGowan, "Ascetism and Early Eucharistic Practice," in Hellholm and Sänger, eds., *The Eucharist*, 836. The term derives from the title of the book by Marcel Detienne and Jean-Pierre Vernant on Greek sacrificial practice.

3. Bachl, *Eucharistie*, 157.

4. Bachl, *Eucharistie*, 150.

5. For the following, see McGowan, "Ascetism and Early Eucharistic Practice," 836.

6. Hippolytus, *Traditio Apostolica*, §6, 48.

7. Joan E. Taylor, *Philo of Alexandria: On the Contemplative Life* (Leiden: Brill, 2020), 73–74.

8. Tatian, *Tatiani Oratio ad Graecos*, 23.

9. Bachl, *Eucharistie*, 75.

10. *Act. Phil.* VIII, 2. See also Bovon, Bouvier, and Amsler, eds., *Acta Philippi*; and the commentary, Amsler, *Acta Philippi* (Belgium: Brepols Publishers NV, 1999).

11. *Acts Phil.* XII, 2.

12. *Acts Phil.* XII, 3.

13. *Acts Phil.* XII, 4–5.

14. *Acts Phil.* XII, 6.

CHAPTER 2

1. For the following, see H. Ulfgard, "Sharing with the Divine in the Apocalypse," in *Old Testament, Early Judaism, New Testament*, vol. 1 of *The Eucharist: Its Origins and Contexts: Sacred Meal, Communal Meal, Table Fellowship in Late Antiquity, Early Judaism, and Early Christianity*, ed. David Hellholm and Dieter Sänger (Tübingen: Mohr Siebeck, 2017), 673–95.

2. "Dû bist mîn, ich bin dîn. Des solt du gewis sîn. Dû bist beslozzen in minem herzen; Verlorn ist daz slüzzelîn: Dû muost

ouch immer darrine sîn" (Hake, Salmann, and Bachl, *Eucharistie*, 84–86).

3. David E. Aune, *Revelation 1—5,* Word Biblical Commentary 52a (Grand Rapids: Zondervan, 2014), 251, 192.

4. The liturgical expansion is based on Ps 118:25, which the crowd greets Jesus with at his entry into Jerusalem (see Matt 21:9).

CHAPTER 3

1. It is unlikely that the prophet John who wrote Revelation is the same John as the Evangelist. "John" was a common name at the time of the New Testament.

2. *Episkopoi* and *diakonoi* are already mentioned together by Paul in Phil 1:1. These are the same Greek words for the later ecclesiastical offices of bishop and deacon. The *presbyteroi* (later "priests") are often mentioned together with *episkopoi* and *diakonoi*, but they do yet appear in the *Didache*. They probably did not yet exist in the churches. See Hippolytus, *Didache: Zwölf-Apostel-Lehre; Traditio Apostolica: Apostolische Überlieferung*, 70–73.

3. See, for example, Eckhard Nordhofen, *Corpora: Die anarchische Kraft des Monotheismus*, 2nd ed. (Freiburg im Breisgau: Herder, 2018), 229–63.

4. Nordhofen, *Corpora*, 241.

5. Gottfried Bachl, *Eucharistie: Macht und Lust des Verzehrens* (Sankt Ottilien: ESO Verlag, 2008), 69.

6. This is also the case in Matt 23:34.

7. Gerhard Lohfink, *Jesus von Nazaret: Was er wollte, wer er war*, 8th ed. (Freiburg im Breisgau: Herder, 2011), 96–98.

8. "To have eaten wisdom with a spoon" (*Weisheit mit Löffeln gefressen*) is a German idiom that refers to one appearing clever, but essentially being a fool. Wisdom cannot be acquired through food.

9. Thomas Ruster, *Wandlung: ein Traktat über Eucharistie und Ökonomie* (Mainz: Matthias Grunewald Verlag, 2009), 143.

10. Ruster, *Wandlung*, 143.

11. Ruster, *Wandlung*, 144.

12. Hippolytus, *Didache*, 69f.

13. Veronika Hoffmann, "Vor Gottes Angesicht treten. Zum Opfer in biblisch-christlicher Perspektive," in *Sühne, Martyrium und Erlösung? Opfergedanke und Glaubensgewissheit in Judentum, Christentum und Islam*, ed. Jürgen Werbick (Leiden, Netherlands: Brill, 2012), 51–71.

14. An antiphon for the feast of Corpus Christi, usually attributed to Aquinas, reads: *O sacrum convivium, in quo Christus sumitur: recolitur memoria passionis eius, mens impletur gratia et futurae gloriae nobis pignus datur. Alleluia*. "O sacred banquet! In which Christ is received, the memory of his Passion is renewed, the mind is filled with grace, and a pledge of future glory to us is given. Hallelujah." Of course, the showbread in the temple makes no christological reference.

15. Bachl, *Eucharistie*, 24.

16. Enrique Dussel, "Das Brot der Feier," in *Herrschaft und Befreiung: Ansatz, Stationen und Themen einer lateinamerikanischen Theologie der Befreiung* (Freiburg, Switzerland: Edition Exodus, 1985), 44–59; "Ökonomie und Eucharistie," *Concilium* 47, no. 5 (2011): 500–510.

17. Dussel, "Das Brot der Feier," 122.

18. Dussel, "Das Brot der Feier," 121.

CHAPTER 4

1. So cautiously Hippolytus, *Didache*, 52; Similarly, Lukas Bormann, "Das Abendmahl: Kulturanthropologische, kognitionswissenschaftliche und ritualwissenschaftliche Perspektiven," in *Old Testament, Early Judaism, New Testament*, vol. 1 of *The Eucharist: Its Origins and Contexts: Sacred Meal, Communal Meal, Table Fellowship in Late Antiquity, Early Judaism, and Early*

Christianity, ed. David Hellholm and Dieter Sänger (Tübingen: Mohr Siebeck, 2017), 697–732. For a very critical reconstructions of the theology of the celebration see: Clemens Leonhard, "Von der Eucharistiefeier zur Messe: Eine Geschichte unumkehrbarer Differenzierung?," *Salzburger Theologische Zeitschrift* 20 (2016): 241. For an overview, see Hans-Ulrich Weidemann, *Taufe und Mahlgemeinschaft: Studien zur Vorgeschichte der altkirchlichen Taufeucharistie* (Tübingen: Mohr Siebeck, 2014).

2. See Rom 14:17: "The kingdom of God is not food and drink but righteousness and peace and joy in the Holy Spirit."

3. See Dietrich-Alex Koch, "Eucharistvollzug und Eucharistieverständnis in der *Didache*," in Hellholm and Sänger, *The Eucharist: Its Origins and Contexts*, 857–58. Koch certainly assumes "that Did. 9-10 is the ritual meal of these communities. It is inaccurate to assume that the ritual action associated with the prayers is incomplete because the so-called words of institution are missing."

4. Hippolytus, *Traditio Apostolica*, 3–4.

5. Norbert Baumert, *Sorgen des Seelsorgers: Übersetzung und Auslegung des ersten Korintherbriefes* (Würzburg: Echter, 2007), 173.

6. Michael Theobald, *Eucharistie als Quelle sozialen Handelns: Eine biblisch-frühkirchliche Besinnung* (Göttingen: Vandenhoeck & Ruprecht, 2012), 72.

7. This is conceivable. See, for example, Phoebe (Rom 16:1–2).

8. Theobald, *Eucharistie als Quelle sozialen Handelns*, 71.

9. Luise Schottroff, *Der Anfang des Neuen Testaments: Matthäus 1-4 neu entdeckt. Ein Kommentar mit Beiträgen zum Gespräch* (Stuttgart: Kohlhammer, 2019), 88.

10. Luise Schottroff, *Der erste Brief an die Gemeinde in Korinth* (Stuttgart: Kohlhammer, 2013), 225.

11. Rudolf Bultmann, *Die Geschichte der synoptischen Tradition*, 8th ed. (Göttingen: Vandenhoeck & Ruprecht, 1970), 286.

12. Schottroff, *Der erste Brief an die Gemeinde in Korinth*, 233.

13. Theobald, *Eucharistie als Quelle sozialen Handelns*, 77.

CHAPTER 5

1. See also Lam 4:4, "The children beg for food [lit. "bread"], / but no one gives [lit. "breaks"] them anything."

2. More information online: https://www.strassenexerzitien.de.

3. See Christian Herwartz, "Der Charme des Anfangs: 'Emmaus'—langsam gelesen (Lk 24,13–36)," *Geist & Leben* 93, no. 2 (2020): 154–60.

4. Herwartz, "Der Charme des Anfangs."

5. Herwartz, "Der Charme des Anfangs."

6. For the following, see Richard Bauckham, "Mary of Clopas," in *Gospel Women. Studies of the Named Women in the Gospels* (Grand Rapids, MI: Wm. B. Eerdmans, 2002), 203–23.

7. For the following, see Daniel Marguerat, "The Meals of Acts," in *Paul in Acts and Paul in His Letters* (Tübingen: Mohr Siebeck, 2013), 157–60.

8. Joseph Ratzinger, "Grundgedanken der eucharistischen Erneuerung des 20. Jahrhunderts," *Klerusblatt* 40 (1960): 208–11.

CONCLUSION

1. Hans Lietzmann, *Die Entstehung der christlichen Liturgie nach den ältesten Quellen* (Darmstadt: Wissenschaftliche Buchgesellschaft, 1963), and *Messe und Herrenmahl: Eine Studie zur Geschichte der Liturgie* (Berlin: De Gruyter, 1967/2012).

2. Volker Leppin and Dorothea Sattler, eds., *Gemeinsam am Tisch des Herrn / Together at the Lord's Table* (Freiburg im Breisgau: Herder, 2020), 4.8.

3. Leppin and Sattler, *Gemeinsam am Tisch des Herrn*, 3.8.5.

4. Barbara Rembser-Mertes and Michael Mertes, eds., *Von der Volkskirche zur Sekte?: Warum die Idee vom Gesundschrumpfen falsch ist* (Paderborn: Bonifatius, 2020), 30.

5. Gottfried Bachl, *Eucharistie: Macht und Lust des Verzehrens* (Sankt Ottilien: ESO Verlag, 2008), 185.

6. See Magdalene L. Frettlöh, "Die Hoffnung schmackhaft machen: Von erlesenen Weinen und dem gefressenen Tod," *Göttinger Predigtmeditationen* 73, no. 2 (2019): 243–50, https://doi.org/10.13109/gpre.2018.73.2.243.

7. Andrea Bieler and Luise Schottroff, *Das Abendmahl: Essen, um zu leben* (Gütersloh & Munich: Gütersloher Verlagshaus, 2007), 17; see Michael Nausner, "Gebrochenheit und Erneuerung der Schöpfung. Das Abendmahl als theologische Basis sozialer Gerechtigkeit," *Ökumenische Rundschau* 61, no. 4, (2012): 440–56.

8. Eckhard Nordhofen, *Corpora: Die anarchische Kraft des Monotheismus*, 2nd ed. (Freiburg im Breisgau: Herder, 2018).